Project Management
an Introduction
BASED ON PRINCE 2®

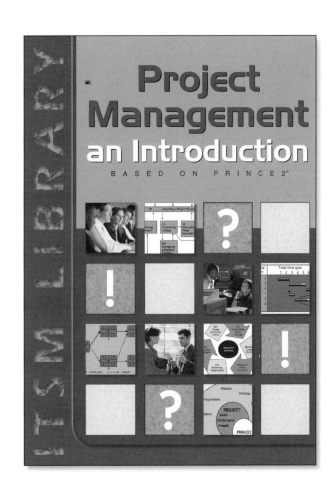

Acknowledgements

Title: Project Management, an Introduction Based on PRINCE2

Version, date: English edition, V1.0, November 2004

Authors: Bert Hedeman (Insights International b.v.), author
                      Hans Fredriksz (ISES International b.v.), author
                      Gabor Vis van Heemst (PinkRoccade b.v.), author

Editors: Jan van Bon (Inform-IT), chief editor
                      Mike Pieper (Inform-IT), editor & final editor

Quality Audit team for the English edition:
                      David Atkinson
                      Colin Bentley (Hampshire Training Consultants)

Quality Audit team for the Dutch edition:
                      Ad van den Akker (Lagant), previewer
                      Rolf Akker (Bureau Hoving & Van Bon)
                      Peter van Gijn (LogicaCMG)
                      Brigit Hendriks (Prince User Group NL)
                      Gerrit Koch (PMI-NL)
                      Martin Liefting (ING OPS&IT)
                      Tanja Muis (Odysseus)
                      Mart van der Niet (Ruysdael)
                      Arie den Ouden (Prince User Group NL)
                      John Roos (ATOSEuronext)
                      Guido Schouten (Good Sense), previewer
                      Ron Seegers (PinkRoccade)
                      Cleo van der Stap (Markov Solutions)
                      Fred Vermeulen (PinkRoccade Educational Services)

Publisher: Van Haren Publishing (info@vanharen.net)
ISBN: 90-77212-31-0
Print: First print, first edition, November 2004
Design & layout: DTPresto Design & Layout, Zeewolde-NL

Foreword

"Project Management, an Introduction Based on PRINCE2" is an extremely useful book about project management and the use of PRINCE2. The authors describe various aspects of project management: covering both the management processes and control of the deliverables, as well as all management roles. The book not only concentrates on the role of the project manager, but also pays a lot of attention to the customer, the suppliers and end users.

The book provides simple, practical examples which reflect the theory. The book is written for anyone with a formal role in the management of projects. It is recommended for customers as well as supplier representatives and users. Even if their departure point in practice is not PRINCE2, this book provides a good reference base.

For the project manager, the book is a 'must'. The inexperienced project managers will profit from the completeness of the PRINCE2 methodology and the various lines of approach to project management practices. More experienced project managers can add to their toolbox and apply this to their own practice. If you close the book and find that you've read nothing new then you deserve a compliment: your management tools won't be the problem.

PRINCE2 is an open methodology. There is room for different techniques like estimates, work planning and risk analysis. This means that many organisations can accommodate their own specific techniques and tools. Besides the fact that it is possible to maintain individual company methods and not hinder collaboration, this means that the transfer to PRINCE2 will not lead to disinvestment.

What is the angle then? Some years ago, research showed that the correlation between project success and the use of methods and techniques was no higher than 30 percent. The rest was determined by the right experience and leadership competency of the project manager. It is the story of the carpenter: you put your trust in someone who has proved himself able to lead your project and in doing so you never look in the tool box. You assume that it's all right. The aim of this book is to contribute to filling this box.

We congratulate the authors Bert Hedeman, Hans Fredriksz and Gabor Vis van Heemst with their book. They have found the time to write about their profession and their experiences with PRINCE2 in a time where the market is demanding additional effort. It characterises the enthusiasm of these three colleagues.

Colin Bentley,

Chief Examiner in PRINCE2 for the Association for Project Management (APM) Group and the OGC.

Gerrit C.L. Koch CPD,

Portfolio holder competency development for the Project Management Institute (PMI) in The Netherlands

Contents

Preface

The book "Project Management, an Introduction" is a practical book for the user working daily on projects. In this book, the process-based approach to project management is described and the components and techniques necessary for this are dealt with.

The description of the processes, components and techniques is based on the PRINCE2 methodology. The same process schedule has been maintained and the same components and techniques are described. The PRINCE2 terminology has also been taken over one to one. This book deals not only with the PRINCE2 methodology, but also with activities and planning resources and the project environment. This complements the PRINCE2 methodology.

In the book's appendices you will find:
• A glossary of terms.
• A setup of the most important management products.
• A health check.
• An example of a detailed Project Brief.
• A filing structure.

The contents of this book largely meet the theoretical requirements set for successfully passing the PRINCE2 Foundation exam. For the PRINCE2 Practitioner exams, however, practical experience is also necessary. A book can never deliver practical experience.

This book does not presume to deal with all the competency areas of project management. For many other competency areas there are numerous books available. It is the area of process-based project management in particular, where a good book for the user is lacking.

This book is written for project managers, project leaders and Team Managers and all other people who privately or in work are involved with the setting up and management of projects. We trust that this book meets the existing need for a useful book in the area of process-based project management.

Finally, we would like to point out that where 'he' or 'his' is used in the book (in reference to persons), 'she' or 'her' can of course be used. All specific PRINCE2 words in this book are written with a capital letter.

We would also like to thank all those who have contributed as reviewers with their comments to this book's quality.

Bert Hedeman, Hans Fredriksz, Gabor Vis van Heemst

1. Introduction to project management

1.1 Why project management?

Managing projects is as old as the hills. There are stories dating back to ancient times about activities we would now call projects. Just think of the mammoth task of the pyramid builders in Egypt and South America. Even the way our forefathers moved encampments from one hunting ground to another can be seen as a project.

The concept of a 'project', however, originated in the 1960s and was mainly applied to major infrastructures. At that time, project management involved little more than planning the work. In the 1970s, attention began being paid to managing the work and after that the personal skills of the project manager came under scrutiny. In the 1990s, attention shifted towards a process-based approach to project management.

Project management is increasingly becoming a profession. Where in the past, project management was a task you took on in addition to your own work, nowadays project management is a separate profession by which many people earn a living. Despite the increased professionalism, projects often fail. Some failed projects hit the headlines, but most are never heard of again. There is no simple reason why projects fail, however, an effective method for managing projects is of vital importance.

Without a project management method, the Executives of a project may have different ideas about organising and completing a project than those who are managing the project and working on it. The people involved do not, for instance, know how much responsibility and authority they have, and thus the project is shrouded in obscurity. Without a project management method, projects are only seldom delivered to the satisfaction of those involved. This particularly applies to projects with a long duration time.

A good project management method must not be static. The environment alters, the market changes, Executives and users take up new positions. In other words, projects have to be managed in a changing environment. Too often, it is assumed that a project can be managed in a 'frozen' environment. That makes things easy, but quickly outdated.

An effective project management method helps the Project Manager to organise and manage a project in a continually changing environment, while still involving all the stakeholders. PRINCE2 is a method that uses the principles of good project management. These principles are:
- A project is a process with a clear beginning and end.
- Projects always have to be managed to be successful.
- To involve stakeholders in the best possible way, they have to know:
  - Why the project is needed.
  - What the aim of the project is.
  - How the result will be achieved.
  - What their responsibilities are.

1.2 What is a project?

It is vitally important to identify the difference between a project and the normal activities that take place within an organisation. Vagueness about what a project actually is, can lead to a lot of friction and frustration. To make the difference between a project and normal activities clear, we have to define what a project is.

1.2.1 Definitions of a project

A frequently used definition is: 'A project is a unique assignment, limited in time and resources, which ends with a project outcome'[1]. And another: 'A project is a unit of cohesive activities, carried out to achieve a previously agreed result, with a time to begin and end, which makes use of limited resources and manpower and is usually one-off by nature[2]'. Although both definitions give specific characteristics of a project, they make no distinction between project activities and the normal activities in an organisation. Many activities in an organisation have a clear beginning and end, make use of a limited quantity of resources and people and produce an agreed result, but they are still not projects.

PRINCE2 describes a project as 'A temporary organisation created for the purpose of delivering one or more business products according to a specified Business Case'. A Business Case is the practical rationale for the development of a product.

> *A project is a temporary organisation created for the purpose of delivering one or more business products according to a specified Business Case.*

This definition adds a new element: working in a temporary organisation. This is exactly what distinguishes a project from the normal activities within an organisation. This is also the reason why working with and in projects is so complicated. A temporary organisation implies that employees are temporarily given a different set of responsibilities and powers. Line management has to delegate certain responsibilities and powers to the project organisation or otherwise a project organisation cannot function properly. This can, however, be threatening to many line managers. The more experience people gain of working in projects, the less significant this threat will become.

1.2.2 Reasons for working in projects

A good reason for carrying out work in the form of a project is that several parties are then involved in the outcome of the project. Such work always involves a change in the status quo for these parties and this almost automatically incites resistance. A temporary project organisation is a good opportunity for guaranteeing a support base and involvement as early as the development phase. Involving the various stakeholders in the set-up and implementation of the project will ensure that the outcome is used. This guarantees that the idea is firmly anchored in the relevant line organisations from an early stage.

The project organisation is temporary; in other words, the project organisation is created for the duration of the project and differs from line management, which is permanent in nature and responsible for the basic activities of the organisation. The style and nature of project management, too, differs from that of line management. These differences can also result in friction and frustration both in the organisations and between them.

The management of a corporate organisation must be aware of the advantages and disadvantages of working in projects and must make conscious decisions in this respect.

---

1 Groote, Geert et al. *Projecten leiden*. Het Spectrum, 2000.
2 Van Aken, Teun. *De weg naar projectsucces*. Reed Business Information, 2002.

1.2.3 Essence of a project

The essence of a project is:
- A temporary organisation.
- An outcome defined in advance.
- The achievement of a result.
- A specified Business Case.

When the project is set up, the Executive and the Project Manager are determined. The other stakeholders are also identified, including the way in which these stakeholders are to be involved in the set-up and management of the project and the achievement of the project outcome.

The project outcome is a product or service that can be delivered. The project outcome must be defined in advance, in outline at the very least. A further specification of the project outcome can be drawn up during the planning of the project itself. The project framework must also be defined. This means that the project definition, the approach, the reasons why the project has to be carried out and sometimes even the outlines of the Project Plan are described, although the latter is not essential.

1.2.4 Relationship between the corporate or programme organisation and projects

Corporate aims can form the basis for the need for a change in the organisation. Projects can be initiated to do this. Sometimes a programme is set up to develop one or more corporate aims (see chapter 6). Programme management then initiates the various projects. Subsequently, the products or services defined are developed in the projects. The project delivers the project outcome to the relevant corporate or programme management. Corporate or programme management is then responsible for ensuring that the aims management had in mind for the outcome are actually achieved through the project outcome. Corporate or programme management, not the project management, is responsible for achieving the corporate aims. The project management is solely responsible for delivering the project outcome with which corporate or programme management can achieve its aims (see figure 1.1).

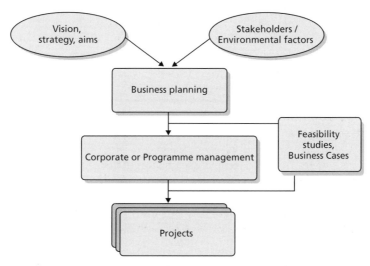

Figure 1.1 Project environment

1.2.5 Aims of a project

The aim of a project is that which corporate or programme management wants to achieve with the outcome the project delivers. This aim must be known before ordering the project to start (see figure 1.2).

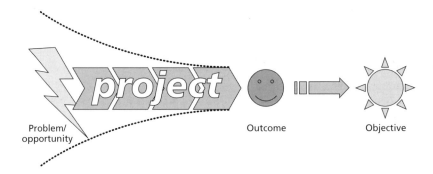

Figure 1.2 Project summary

1.2.6 The difference between a product lifecycle and a project lifecycle

To be able to define responsibilities, it is important to understand the difference between the lifecycle of a product and that of a project.

The lifecycle of a product begins with the idea for the product and continues on through its development and use until the product is discontinued. The lifecycle of a project is much more limited. The lifecycle of a project begins with the specification and continues on through development and testing to its implementation (see figure 1.3).

The first phase, that of forming ideas and carrying out a feasibility study, and the final phase, use and ultimate discontinuation, are not part of the lifecycle of a project. The project organisation cannot take any responsibility for these phases, as they are in the hands of the corporate or programme management.

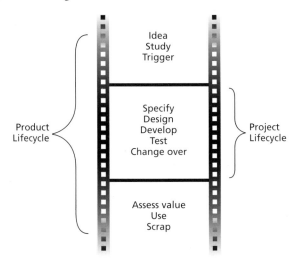

Figure 1.3 Product lifecycle and project lifecycle (Source: OGC)

If a study is first required to examine what needs to happen, the best approach is to treat this study as a separate project and then to set up a new project to develop the results of the study.

Several projects can be carried out during the lifecycle of a product. In addition to the feasibility study and the development project there are often interim revisions and 'upgrades' carried out in the form of a project and, in the same way, both the discontinuation and the replacement of the product as well as its economic lifecycle come to an end.

1.3 What is a successful project?

In the last few years there have been regular discussions about the results recorded with the use of projects. Not so long ago, enormous investments were made in IT projects that promised the earth. Many of these projects were unable to fulfil their promise and there were increasingly strident calls for a critical look to be taken at the results actually achieved.

But this is also the case in other sectors. Research results are regularly published showing that many projects are completed too late and/or are too expensive. There have also been situations in which a project is concluded prematurely without producing any result or projects whose outcome is never used in practice. How does this happen? So much experience has been gathered about carrying out projects. Where do projects go wrong? And furthermore, what are the factors that ought to be taken into account to complete a project successfully?

In the first place, it is important to have a common definition of the success of a project. Opinion is divided on this. The Netherlands Competence Baseline (NCB) describes it as follows: 'the success of a project is the extent to which, in the opinion of the Executive, the intended result corresponds to the actual result delivered'. Teun van Aken's definition of the success of a project: 'if all the parties involved are satisfied with the outcome'[3].

> *A project is successful if all the parties involved are satisfied with the result achieved.*

Teun van Aken's definition clearly goes further than that of the NCB. If only the Executive is satisfied with the result, but not the users, for example, then the project cannot be called successful. If the users are dissatisfied about the results of the project, they will not be inclined to get the maximum return from the product (or service) that has been delivered.

The term 'all parties' in the definition above covers:
• The Executive
• The users
• The suppliers
• The project staff

The Executive is the one who wants to get certain benefits from the project outcome and is the one who pays for it. The users are those who will have to work with the outcome. These may be end users, but could also be the people who are responsible for management and maintenance. The suppliers supply the people and resources needed to produce the outcome. The project staff consists of those who have worked on producing the outcome. In practice, the users are the most important factor when it comes to determining the extent to which a project has been successful, followed by the Executive and subsequently the suppliers and the staff.

---

3 Van Aken, Teun. *De weg naar projectsucces*. Reed Business Information, 2002.

So we see that there are several parties that determine the success of a project. It is therefore essential throughout the entire project to look at the stakeholders and the criteria for success that they employ. These can be entirely different for each one of them and can differ from project to project. The absence of factors that one of the stakeholders considers to be important can be a reason for loss of motivation and for halting the project. Possible success factors for the various stakeholders are:

- The benefits of the project outcome exceed the cost of the project and are in line with expectations -> Executive.
- The outcome meets the criteria laid down in advance and is 'fit for use' -> users.
- A positive return on spending -> supplier.
- The work is enjoyable and contributes to personal development -> project staff.

1.4 Why do projects fail?

Some of the reasons given for the failure of projects are:
- The lack of a clear Business Case.
- A lack of involvement on the part of the Executive.
- Not having a clear outcome or an outcome that has been defined in insufficient detail.
- The lack of acceptance criteria.
- The lack of quality criteria and checks.
- Changing specifications or the lack of efficient change control.
- A lack of involvement on the part of the user from the start of the project.

A clear **Business Case** forms the basis for a project. After all, this is where the Executive gives his reasons for having the project carried out. If it is not sufficiently clear, it may be that the Executive will reduce his **involvement** during the course of the project because it is no longer clear what the project will contribute to his corporate aims. If the Business Case is not clear and explicit from the start, the users too can cause problems as soon as they realise what the project will mean to them. The withdrawal of involvement on the part of the Executive will likewise give the project staff the feeling that their activities are unimportant.

Another issue is that of an insufficiently **defined outcome**. How can you make something satisfactorily if you do not know what your Executive or the user wants? It is important here too that not only **quality criteria** are drawn up for the deliverables, but that the **Acceptance Criteria** are described. The better all this is described, the more realistically the costs can be estimated in the Business Case and the better the consequences of any **changes** can be calculated. It is therefore important that both the Executive and the user are involved throughout the project.

1.5 Context & scope of PRINCE2

Project management consists of a number of aspects that, when placed in the correct context and balance, deliver an outcome that can justifiably be called a successful project. These aspects are the 'I-we-they-it' aspects of project management (see figure 1.4).

The extent to which a project is successful heavily depends on the personal qualities of the Project Manager. The Project Manager provides leadership, drives and gives direction. The personal qualities of the Project Manager are the **I-aspects**.

In addition to this, the Project Manager is the catalyst and facilitator for assembling teams and is responsible for the best possible team spirit and motivation. These are the **we-aspects**.

The Project Manager must be able to deal with the various stakeholders in the project: the Executive, the users, the suppliers, and with parties like environmental pressure groups, local residents and others. The Project Manager must understand the field of influence in and around the project and must be able to deal effectively with it. To do this, he must focus continuously on the environment and take account of the stakeholders' increasing understanding. He ensures that there is a support base and matches the company culture to the approach to the project. These are the **they-aspects**.

Last but not least there are the **it-aspects** of project management. These comprise not only the methodology and the procedures, the tools and techniques, but also aspects like know-how, knowledge of the sector, knowledge of purchasing, legal issues and suchlike. These also include all the coordination and organisation in a project. All agreements about the systems, structures and procedures to be used are recorded in a methodology or action plans.

This book mainly deals with the it-side of project management, based on the project management methodology PRINCE2. PRINCE2 focuses on the management of projects and on the project in its environment. PRINCE2 is not intended to cover all the aspects of project management. Social and communication skills, techniques, software support packages and technical activities are not covered by the scope of PRINCE2. At the same time this is the strength of the methodology. PRINCE2 is not bound to its own specification of these aspects, which enables the methodology to be used for all projects and in all types of organisations.

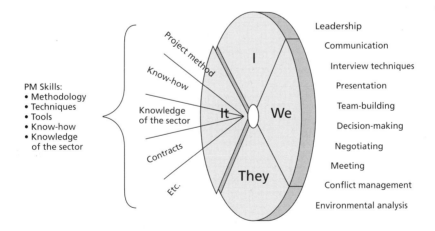

Figure 1.4 I-we-they-it of project management

People always need social and communication skills. These are not limited to the project environment, but are just as important in the line organisation. These skills are essential for all people, both at home and at work. PRINCE2 recognises that these skills are essential for the management of projects ('make it happen'), but realises that these skills are firmly tied to individuals and situations and makes no comment on them.

Project management is the work of people. PRINCE2 cannot be used like a recipe book. PRINCE2 has to be used in combination with common sense and the right technical and social skills. Interaction is an important component of PRINCE2. It is bound up in the tasks, responsibilities and powers of the roles in a project. Because these roles have been made explicit, management is easier and people can be called to account for their responsibilities.

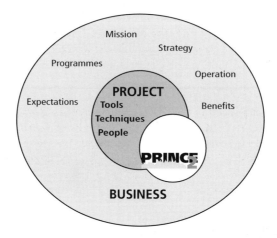

Figure 1.5 Scope of PRINCE2 (Source: OGC)

PRINCE2 comprises three management techniques:
- Product-based planning
- Change control approach
- Quality review technique

Other techniques and software support packages that can be used vary tremendously for each type of project and organisational environment and are often company-dependent. A fourth technique has been added in this book, namely 'Planning of activities and resources'.

PRINCE2 deals with project management and the management of resources to be deployed in undertaking the project. PRINCE2 makes no comment about the design approach to be used. This can be different for each project.

Another important aspect involves the purchase and acquisition of resources. PRINCE2 assumes that the project is being carried out within the boundaries of a contract. This 'contracting process' is not part of the method, but is one of the technical activities that can be carried out using PRINCE2.

2. Introduction to PRINCE2

2.1 What is PRINCE2

PRINCE was designed in 1989 by the former CCTA (Central Computer and Telecommunication Agency). It is based on PROMPT II, a project management method developed in 1975 by Simpact Systems Ltd. and used by the British government. PRINCE is a project management method and stands for 'Projects In Controlled Environments'. PRINCE has followed PROMPTII as the de-facto standard for the British Government. Today PRINCE2 is in the hands of the OGC (Office of Government Commerce) that has registered it as a trademark.

PRINCE was directed at projects in the IT sector in particular and was not suitable for use in other sectors. Therefore, in 1996, PRINCE2 was introduced, where the methodology was adapted in order to make it suitable for every project type, in every environment and at every level. Internationally, PRINCE2 became used increasingly as the method for managing projects. The OGC owns the copyright of the trademark PRINCE2 and the PRINCE2 methodology, but the method is free for individual use.

2.2 PRINCE2 assumptions

There are four assumptions for PRINCE2 that form the basis of the complete method.

1. **Projects are carried out in a changing environment** - the market changes, the internal organisation changes, users' insight increases, etc. Projects initiate changes and these changes again affect the project. Projects must be set up such that they can anticipate change in a controlled manner. The setting of a task at the start of the project is not a criterion, but the expectations of the end of the project. When setting up and managing a project, explicit account must also be taken of this.

2. **A project is only successful if all stakeholder parties are satisfied with the project outcome** - stakeholder parties are the users, the Executive, the suppliers and the project employees. It is often not sufficient to supply that which was originally agreed on time and within budget. Not only the opinion of the Executive plays a role, but the experience of all stakeholder parties. Managing the expectations of the stakeholder parties is therefore also an extremely advisable part of project management.

3. **Successful projects are 'business driven'** - there must be a basic business requirement for carrying out a project. This basic business requirement (Business Case) must be set at the start of the project. Regular checking of the basic business requirement must take place as the project progresses. If there is not a clear basic business requirement, this will almost certainly form an obstacle for maintaining the involvement of management, generating the necessary funds and 'promoting' the project in the environment. The Business Case gives the framework within which users specify their wishes and requirements with regard to the use and maintenance of the result to be delivered.

4. **Cooperation of all stakeholder parties in the project leads to more successful projects** - projects are setup in order to implement change. Cooperation is an essential factor in this. If all parties are involved in the setup and management of the project, the acceptance of the outcome will almost always be higher than when that is not the case.

These four assumptions affect the setup and management of projects and are translated into the organisation of a project, the project processes to be carried out and the components and techniques to be applied.

2.3 PRINCE2 characteristics

PRINCE2 distinguishes itself in a number of ways from other project management methods:

- **The creation of stakeholder involvement at project management level** - besides the involvement of users and suppliers in the implementation of a project, it is important that the users and the supplier are also represented at project management level. Good communication between all stakeholder parties is essential for the 'commitment' between these parties. PRINCE2 interprets this by including the users and suppliers as representatives on the Project Board in the role of Senior User and Senior Supplier.

- **Focus on justification (Business Case)** - the Business Case forms the justification for undertaking the project. The Business Case forms the basis for starting and carrying out a project. The Business Case is also updated with every no go/go decision of the Project Board. After the project outcome has been delivered and put into service, an evaluation takes place to determine whether the project outcome corresponds with what the Customer had in mind.

- **Management of risk completely integrated into the life cycle of the project** - management of risk within PRINCE2 is not in itself an independent approach but is an integral part of the PRINCE2 management process. It indicates precisely who carries out a risk analysis when, and who carries out activities as well as those involved.

- **A defined organisation structure** - characteristic of a project is that it consists of a temporary organisational form. The project is setup to bring about change. It is not simply the intention to perform tasks as effectively and efficiently as possible, but also, during the project, to create a basis for the outcome and for the change that must be carried out. In order to achieve this, a broad grounding of the project is necessary within the line organisations involved, and clear and unequivocal agreements are necessary about who does what and who is responsible. PRINCE2 provides a defined organisational structure in order to determine an individual project's organisation.

- **Division between technique and management** - PRINCE2 divides tasks, responsibilities and authority within the various roles of a project organisation, a division between technique and management. The Project Manager is responsible for the daily management of the project, within the framework provided by the Project Board, and is therefore responsible for the process in place of the content. The various Team Managers are responsible for putting into practice the agreed products according to the agreed content specifications, time and budget.

- **A controlled start, middle and end** - projects are often started too quickly. During the project people focus too much on what they have to do, but not on working according to the agreement. The termination of a project and the hand-over of the outcome to the line organisation are often unclear. These important reasons are why projects fail. PRINCE2 assumes a controlled start, whereby the project, the project organisation and the first tasks to be carried out are clearly and well defined, before starting with the project itself. During the project the Project Manager has the daily management of the project within the framework provided by the Project Board. With the closure of the project the Project Manager must not only ensure that the outcome is delivered, but that the projection organisation is also disbanded, that the project is properly evaluated and closed, that the outstanding actions are delivered to the line organisations involved and that a date and plan is set for a post-project review.

- **'Management by exception' by the Project Board** - PRINCE2 employs this principle. The Project Board do not need to meet to receive updates on progress, rather they receive regular Highlight Reports at a frequency which they decide. This characterises the 'best practice' character of PRINCE2. If an "exception" situation arises then the Project Board will be informed via an Exception Report. At the end of a stage the Project Board receive an End Stage Report. This does not mean, however, that regularly planned meetings do not take place.

- **Management stages** - PRINCE2 distinguishes management stages and technical stages.

Management stages are divisions in time coupled with an explicit no go/go decision about the progress of the project. The setup of management stages is an important part of putting 'management by exception' into practice.

- **Instruments for managing the commitment of people and resources** - often a budget is available for a project but the project cannot start or go any further because the necessary people and resources are not made available or because people and resources are taken off the project. PRINCE2 links the authorisation to carry out work in the next stage to the actual availability of the required people and resources. Management stages ensure that the Project Board commit the necessary people and resources required for the next stage.
- **Contracting out based on Work Packages** - work that must be carried out by Team Managers is directed based on Work Packages. This applies both to the internal activities and to the activities that must be carried out by third parties. Work Packages give a defined description of the products to be supplied and the necessary information important for the development of these products, the assessments to be carried out, the interim reports, process management and the manner in which the products realised must finally be delivered.
- **Product-based planning** - product-based planning is typical of result-based thinking and working in projects. As a basis for the various plans this PRINCE2 technique forces all those involved to base their thinking on the deliverables: what is to be delivered (possibly early) and what requirements must it meet? From this the necessary activities are planned for developing the products.
- **Quality reviews** - if the products to be developed are only tested at the point of delivery, it is too late to make adjustments to the quality of the product. The most important decisions for determining the end quality of the product are taken at the start of the project. The documents required for these decisions must therefore be critically checked with the question: to what extent does what is laid down in these documents actually lead to that which must be achieved? The quality review is a technique for the controlled evaluation of documents and other products.
- **Controlling change is managed in the PRINCE2 method** - PRINCE2 assumes that projects do not stand in isolation, but must be managed in a changing environment. It is therefore also logical that change control is an essential part of PRINCE2 and completely embedded in the methodology.

2.4 PRINCE2 advantages

PRINCE2 is a methodology that gives **directors and managers** of projects the advantage through better control of the commitment of people and resources. They are continually kept up to date on the progress and can limit themselves to managing exceptions. PRINCE2 stimulates active involvement of the user and the stakeholders throughout the complete project with an integrated and structured approach to changes and risks. PRINCE2 has a project organisation in which roles are defined with clear agreements for tasks, authority and responsibilities.

For the **company management and the project Executives** the focus is on the added value for the organisation, management of company risks and the hold on current projects which is valuable, both at the start of a project and during its execution.

The combination of a thorough theoretical basis with 'best practices', a process-based approach and intensive participation of users, appeals to **project management**. The Project Manager is able to employ a set structure for delegation, authorisation and communication based on

PRINCE2. PRINCE2 provides a clear structure divided into manageable stages, coupled with the allocation of the people and resources to execute the work. Furthermore, PRINCE2 provides a transparent reporting structure, so that management and stakeholder meetings can be limited to a minimum.

For the **supplier** it is important that PRINCE2 is a standard project management methodology with uniform terminology, structure and 'templates'. This increases the quality of the service and eases the possible exchange of Project Managers or employees due to sickness or absence. PRINCE2 forms a good base for ensuring the quality of the project management process and for professional project management in the organisation. The method is free for individual use. The international PRINCE2 training and certification is also considered as important.

The **users** are involved from the start with the decision-making in the project. The users are responsible for the quality requirements within the framework of the Business Case and take part in quality assessments (quality reviews) throughout the project.

For **those executing the work/Team Managers** in the project the method gives a clear description of the Work Package to be carried out and all the relevant information and agreements. This gives a clear division of tasks, responsibilities and the authority of the Project Manager and the Team Manager and the work area of the Team Manager is defined.

PRINCE2 can be used for all projects. The method can be scaled and adjusted to every specific circumstance within which a project must be carried out. This does not mean that parts of the process are missed, but that the processes can be run through more or less explicitly and more or less documented.

2.5 PRINCE2 overview

PRINCE2 is a structured project management method based on best practice. PRINCE2 has a process-based setup, which means that the method assumes that a project is carried out as a process rather than in a linear form. Some processes are in principle only gone through once in a project, other processes may be gone through more times. This depends upon the size, complexity and setup of the project.

In addition, PRINCE2 has eight components and three techniques. This book contains a fourth technique: the Planning of Activities and Resources is added to the three PRINCE2 techniques. Figure 2.1 gives an overview of the processes and components.

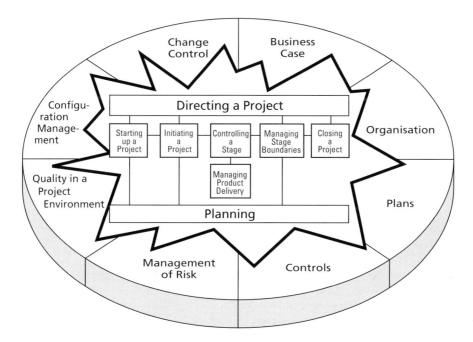

Figure 2.1 Processes and components (Source: OGC)

2.5.1 Processes

The PRINCE2 processes cover the complete route from the start up of a project through controlling and managing progress, to the conclusion of the project. In chapter 3 of this book the processes are expanded and explained in detail.

- **Starting Up a Project (SU)** - this is the first PRINCE2 process. It has the objective of creating all the conditions for starting a project. During this process the Project Brief, provisional project organisation, Project Approach, Risk Log and a Planning for the initiation stage are produced.
- **Directing a Project (DP)** - this process runs throughout the duration of the project - from project preparation to delivery and Closing a Project. Directing a Project describes the processes used by the Project Board. The process focuses on maximising the chance of a successful project and delivers what the customer and the user expect, as well as taking important decisions for the project.
- **Initiating a Project (IP)** - this process describes the definition stage of the project and indicates how the Project Initiation Document (PID) is worked out in detail and set up, so that the Project Board can decide whether to implement the project. The PID also gives the basis for executing the project and provides the foundation for controlling the project progress. This process is the first process in the project and begins after the Project Board has approved the execution of the initiation stage.
- **Controlling a Stage (CS)** - this process describes the daily management by the Project Manager during a stage. This process begins when the people and resources are made available for the stage and the Stage Plan has been approved by the Project Board. This process is aimed at the delivery of the agreed products within the previously determined tolerances. This process is essential for the project's success.
- **Managing Product Delivery (MP)** - this process makes it possible for the Team Managers to reach an agreement with the Project Manager about the work to be carried out, in order to

plan and execute the work as well as supplying the complete Work Package to the Project Manager. This process must be approached carefully in order to avoid bureaucracy.

- **Managing Stage Boundaries (SB)** - the aim of this process is to review the previous stage and plan the next to enable the Project Board to take a no go/go decision about the progress of the project. This process gives the Project Board the security that the products in the current stage have been delivered according to plan, gives the Stage Plan for the next stage and indicates the consequences for the Project Plan and the Business Case.
- **Closing a Project (CP)** - if all project objectives have been met or if the Project Board has decided to prematurely end a project, the process Closing a Project checks the extent to which the objectives set out in the PID have been met. The project is also closed and documentation archived so that an audit can be carried out later. In this process recommendations are also set for any subsequent actions and the End Project Report and the Lessons Learned Report are produced.
- **Planning (PL)** - the Planning process supports many other processes. A plan is not only a time schedule, but a document that describes how, when and by whom a specific objective or result must be reached and the consequences for time, money and quality.

2.5.2 Components

The components are the ingredients of the project that the Project Manager needs to manage with the processes. Chapter 4 describes and explains the components in detail.

- **Business Case** - the Business Case gives an overview of the costs and benefits of a project, or the basic business requirement. This gives the reason for executing the project. PRINCE2 calls this the added value of a project or rather the driving force behind the project.
- **Organisation** - PRINCE2 provides an organisational structure for the Project Management Team with the job descriptions, tasks, authority, and responsibilities as well as their interrelationships. The roles can be combined or divided depending upon the size of the project.
- **Plans** - within PRINCE2 a number of levels are defined for planning that depending upon the size and complexity can be adapted to the project's requirements. PRINCE2 assumes a plan is based on the deliverables.
- **Controls** - using a number of controls, each level can be measured against how the project is progressing. Progress is compared with the plans made and provides an input for decision-making. Controls are applied throughout the project to ensure that the project is carried out in a controlled manner from the start to the delivery of required products.
- **Management of Risk** - PRINCE2 defines a risk as "uncertainty about the future". Risks must be identified and evaluated. Effective measures must be taken in order to avoid risks. Risks must be managed throughout the project. PRINCE2 defines a number of key moments when risk analysis can be carried out and provides indications for risk analysis and controlling risks.
- **Quality in a Project Environment** - quality plays an important part in a PRINCE2 project and is a fully integrated part of the method. Quality is assessed for both the processes and the products. The basis for quality control is set at the start of the project by the customer's quality expectations and acceptation criteria by the representative of the user organisation.
- **Configuration Management** - all products that are produced must be followed throughout the duration of the project. Configuration Management enables the Project Manager to set the status, content and location of products at any time and to check who has access to these products.
- **Change Control** - changes in the size of the project or in the product specifications can considerably affect a project (in costs and time). It is important to implement structured changes and to know the consequences for the project and the Business Case.

2.5.3 Techniques

PRINCE2 describes the techniques Product-based planning, the Change control approach and Quality review. This book, in addition to discussing these three techniques, also includes a technique for Planning of activities and resources. The authors of this book view this as an important aid when going through the Planning process. In chapter 5, the techniques are elaborated upon and explained in detail.

- **Product-based planning** - PRINCE2 provides for a product-based approach to planning, before a start is made with on planning activities. The product-based planning technique is divided into three steps: Producing a Product Breakdown Structure, Writing Product Descriptions, and Producing a Product Flow Diagram.
- **Planning of activities and resources** - in the Netherlands, the Precedence network method is usually used for planning activities. Planning this network is converted into a Gantt chart, from which finally the people and resources needed are properly planned.
- **Change control approach** - the technique Change control approach provides the procedure for managing change. In PRINCE2 all potential changes are treated as Project Issues. These may be raised at any time during the project. PRINCE2 makes a distinction between A Request for Change, An Off-Specification and other Project Issues, such as a change in the project environment.
- **Quality review** - a quality review is a structured procedure for assessing the quality of products, in particular, subjective quality criteria and ensuring that these meet the expectations of the users.

2.6 PRINCE2 terminology

All terms characteristic to PRINCE2 are explained in the glossary of terms at the back of the book (see appendix 7.1). There are, however a number of terms that are most important for understanding the PRINCE2 method:

- **Business Case** - information that justifies the setting up, continuation or termination of the project. The Business Case answers the question: "Why this project should be done?" The Business Case is monitored and updated throughout the project.
- **Project Board** - the platform that is finally responsible for the project. The Project Board is made up of representatives from the customer, the users and the supplier. The Project Board is chaired by the Executive, who is chairman of the Project Group.
- **Customer** - the person or group, who has commissioned the project, invested in the project and will benefit from the project.
- **User** - anyone who will be influenced by the outcome. They are the ones who will work with it, take the product produced with the help of the project outcome, who must reach their objective with the project outcome, be troubled or helped by the project outcome and who must maintain the project outcome.
- **Supplier** - those who are responsible for providing the people and resources to the project and responsible for creating the project outcome.
- **Product, end product or outcome** - is used for everything that the project must deliver. The Project outcome can vary enormously from physical items, such as buildings and machinery, to intangible things such as culture change and public perception.

3. Processes

3.1 Introduction to processes

3.1.1 Why a process-based approach?
In order to manage a project it is wise to approach the project as a process. A process approach provides the possibility of controlling the project under changing circumstances. The process approach is embraced by all modern project management methods.

3.1.2 Four management levels
Process management according to PRINCE2 is based on the presence of 4 management levels: three management levels in the project itself and the corporate or programme management. Each management level has its own specific role:

- **Corporate or programme management** - this is the coordinating level. The corporate or programme management does not take part in the project itself, but does define the corporate or programme objectives that justify the project. The corporate or programme management also uses the project outcome and uses this to execute the planned corporate activities and achieve the projected benefits.
- **Project Board** - this is the highest management level in a project. The Project Board is chaired by the Executive. The Executive is the person responsible for the customer's corporate or programme management in the project and is ultimately responsible for the project, to the same corporate or programme management. The Project Board takes all the important decisions concerning the project and directs and leads the project as a whole.
- **Project Manager** - is responsible for the daily management of the project, for directing the Team Managers and for the preparation of the decision-making of the Project Board. The Project Manager is responsible for the project within the framework set by the Project Board.
- **Team Manager** - is responsible for the final development of the products defined by the project. The Team Manager directs the team members.

Of course, for successful closure of the project, it is important that the various management levels communicate properly.

Different roles/levels can be combined in a small project: for example the corporate or programme manager and the Executive can be one and the same person, or the Project and Team Manager can also be one and the same person. For the description of the process methodology this does not matter. For individual projects, the various subprocesses can be combined in such cases. In paragraph 3.10 of this chapter managing small and/or informal projects will be dealt with separately.

3.1.3 The management processes
In order to manage a project, eight main processes are defined. They are divided based on the different stages within a project and the different responsibilities (see figure 3.1).

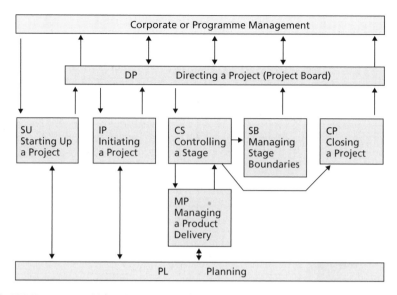

Figure 3.1 The PRINCE2 Process Model (Based on: OGC source)

Each process is again divided into a number of subprocesses. Some processes take place once and other processes may take place more frequently within a project.

3.1.4 PRINCE2 processes in a time framework

A project has a minimum of two management stages: the initiation stage ("thinking") and the execution stage ("doing"). Execution covers all specialist work in order to achieve a project outcome, such as design, work preparation, realisation and implementation. The execution stage can be divided into more management stages.

Before the project can be started a number of matters must be arranged in a pre-project stage. This gives the following arrangement:

- **Pre-project stage** - in this stage the project organisation is determined and the Project Brief and initiation stage plan setup. These activities take place in the process Starting Up a Project (SU).
- **Initiation stage** - once the decision has been made to start the project, all information describing how the plan will be executed must be collected and a plan made about how and when the project outcome will be delivered. In the initiation stage, the processes Initiating a Project (IP) and Managing Stage Boundaries (SB) take place once. Managing the stage boundaries of the initiation stage for the (first) execution stage must be done in the same way as the transition from one execution stage to the next.
- **Execution stage (s)** - execution of what is agreed in the initiation stage. In the execution stages the processes Controlling a Stage (CS), Managing a Product Delivery (MP), Managing Stage Boundaries (SB) and Closing a Project (CP) take place.

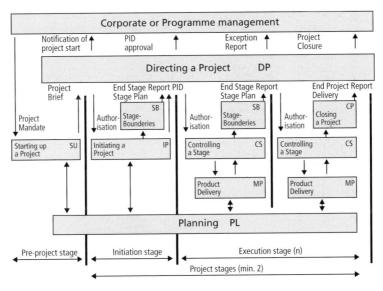

Figure 3.2 Processes in a time frame

The processes Directing a Project (DP) and Planning (PL) take place in all of the various stages.

3.1.5 The structure of the process descriptions

Each process will be described in the following paragraphs in a fixed order:

- **Context** - gives the relationship between the process
  - and other processes and
  - the project environment.
- **Fundamental principles**
  - Why is the process concerned necessary?
  - What has to be achieved during the process?
  - Why is this process necessary for good project management?
- **Process description** - describes how the objectives of the process are achieved. Although there is usually no strict sequence for the activities, the activities will be described in an order that is as logical as possible.
- **Input and output** - gives an overview of all management products that are needed per subprocess, and which management products are created or actualised per subprocess.
- **Responsibilities** - indicates who in the Project Management Team is responsible for a certain activity in the process.

Each project must go through all the processes of the process model. The extent depends upon the size, duration time and complexity of the project. Also important is whether the project will be carried out with in-house people only or using third parties. Finally, it is important whether the project is part of a larger project or programme or not. At the end of this chapter, managing small and/or informal projects will be dealt with. Chapter 6 deals with managing projects within a programme.

3.2 Starting Up a Project (SU)

3.2.1 Context
The process Starting Up a Project is conducted in the pre-project stage of a project, before the actual start of the project, and is relatively short compared with the total duration of a project. The project begins once this process has been gone through and the Project Board has authorised the start of the project. Based on the results of this process, the next processes Initiating a Project starts.

The process Starting Up a Project is started upon receipt of a request to start the project. This request must give the reasons for the project and what the customer wishes to achieve with the project. This request from the customer is called in PRINCE2 terms a Project Mandate. The Project Mandate is often set up by the corporate or programme management of the customer.

The Project Mandate may be a substantial document, but it can also be a verbal request or notes on the back of a cigarette box. If the future project is part of a programme, the Project Mandate often contains the complete content of a Project Brief.

The process Starting Up a Project starts with the corporate or programme management appointing the Executive and the Project Manager (SU1). They put the Project Management Team together (SU2), after which the appointment of individuals for the various roles within the Project Management Team takes place (SU3). The Project Brief and the Risk Log are prepared (SU4). Subsequently the Project Approach is defined (SU5) and finally, the Stage Plan for the initiation stage is set up (SU6) (see figure 3.3).

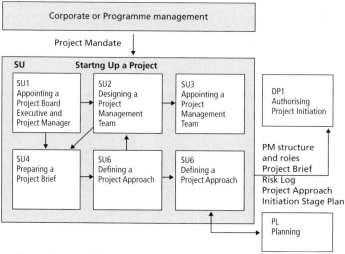

Figure 3.3 Starting Up a Project (Based on: OGC source)

3.2.2 Fundamental principles
The Fundamental principles for the SU process are:
- There must be a Business Case in order to start the project (is the project viable?).
- Certain information is needed in order to be able to make a rational decision on starting a project.
- No activities can be carried out before the responsibilities have been defined and roles filled.
- Before approval can be given to start with the initiation stage an Initiation Stage Plan must be formulated.

If there is not a basic business requirement for triggering the start of the project, it should not be started. If it is not clear why a project is required for the organisation, there is little chance of the project being successful. The lack of a good Business Case is one of the most important factors for the failure of projects.

Certain information is needed in order to be able to start the initiation stage. The various parties are already involved in the project at this stage and costs are incurred by them for the project. If it is not clear what the Executive wishes to achieve with the project at the start of the initiation stage, the various parties will work according to a variety of perspectives in this initiation stage. This can lead to friction and frustration, the ineffective employment of people and resources, and a bad basic document for the execution of the project.

At least one Executive and one Project Manager are needed who together agree to develop the project. The other Project Board members must also be appointed in this stage of the project.

A plan must be set up for all the activities. This also applies to the activities to be carried out in the initiation stage. The users and suppliers are involved in the initiation stage. What is done by whom, when and how, as well as the detail to which it must be done is agreed. It is necessary to plan commitment, and work agreements must be made. Otherwise the project will fall apart before it has even started.

3.2.3 Process description
The objective of the process Starting Up a Project is to ensure a structured and controlled start to the project. This means that:
- All rolls in the project have been identified and the tasks, responsibilities and authorities defined.
- The project definition and the framework within which the project must be developed has been determined.
- The work for carrying out the process Initiating a Project is planned and assigned.
- The organisation that must host the project team is informed and knows which facilities will be affected.

The activities of the Starting Up a Project process are:
- Design and appoint the Project Management Team.
- Take care of the project definition and the framework within which the project must be carried out, preferably in the form of a Project Brief.
- Establish an agreed Project Approach with the stakeholder parties.
- Set up a Risk Log based upon the most important initial risks.
- Create the Initiation Stage Plan.

Appointing a Project Board Executive and Project Manager (SU1)
First of all the corporate or programme management will appoint the Project Board Executive and the Project Manager. Their tasks, responsibilities and authorities will be defined and agreed. It is recommended that the corporate or programme management confirm their appointment and job descriptions.

Use is made of the Project Mandate with the appointment of the Executive and the Project Manager. SU1 gives the agreed job descriptions of the Executive and the Project Manager.

Designing a Project Management Team (SU2)

The right person in the right place. That sounds simple, but it is not. The people in the Project Management Team must have not only the right know-how but also sufficient authority and responsibility to be able to make the right decisions in a timely manner. The Project Management Team composition must evenly reflect the interests of all stakeholder parties.

> *The Project Management Team encompasses the complete management structure of the Project Board, Project Manager, Team Managers, Project Support and Project Assurance roles.*

The composition of the Project Board is of particular importance. Take stock of the interests, design a possible Project Board, and assess whether certain tasks of the Project Board need to be delegated to a separate Project Assurance. Examine whether separate Team Managers must be appointed, determine job descriptions and select candidates for the separate roles.

SU2 overlaps a lot with the subsequent process of appointing a Project Management Team. It is, however, essential to separate both processes. It often becomes apparent that the people available are not right for a specific role within the Project Management Team. In practice, it is extremely difficult to pass over explicitly nominated persons. These situations can be avoided by having a draft Project Management Team and relevant job descriptions.

When designing a Project Management Team use is made of the Project Mandate and the job descriptions of the Executive and the Project Manager. SU2 delivers the draft for the Project Management Team with the draft job descriptions and (a list of) possible candidates for the various roles.

Appointing a Project Management Team (SU3)

It is essential that all members of the Project Management Team know their roles, tasks, responsibilities and authorities, and what the communication and reporting lines are. This is clearly discussed, agreed and laid down with the members of the Project Management Team. There should be no overlap between the various roles. The appointment of the members of the Project Management Team and their job descriptions are confirmed by corporate or programme management.

SU3 makes use of the results from SU2. The output of the process is an approved and agreed Project Management Team, with the relevant job descriptions.

Preparing a Project Brief (SU4)

The Project Brief is an important document for starting a project. The Project Board members must be satisfied that the project is viable. It is important that all Project Board members and the Project Manager endorse the Project Brief. The Project Brief must be discussed with all the interested parties. This is essential for creating a support-base for good management expectations.

The Project Mandate is the basis for the Project Brief. It is possible that the information given in the Project Mandate needs to be updated. The Project Brief gives the project definition and a framework outline within which the project must be carried out. The quality expectations and Acceptance Criteria of the customer (functional specification) must be determined in this stage, as well as the most important risks. These form part of the Project Brief. The Risk Log is created, including the risks given in the Project Brief. For a Project Brief and Risk Log setup see appendix 7.2.22 and 7.2.30.

This process is also essential if the project is part of a programme and the programme already has a completely defined Project Brief. It may be necessary to adapt or work out parts of the Project Brief. Changes and additions to the Project Brief must, of course, be discussed and agreed with the management of the programme.

SU4 uses the project mandate and delivers the draft Project Brief and the initial Risk Log.

Project Brief

- Background:
  - Context of the project: description of the project environment.
  - Reason to start the project: that there may be a problem or a possibility of a problem.
- Project definition:
  - Project objectives: what the Executive wishes to achieve.
  - Scope (range): both regarding content (activities) and the size (parts involved).
  - Most important project outcomes: outline of project deliverables and/or desired outcomes.
  - Exclusions: that which does not belong to the project, both regarding the objectives, results and scope.
  - Constraints: the limitations within which the project must be developed.
  - Relations with other projects: both the dependences regarding products and the critical commitment of people and resources.
- Outline the Business Case:
  - A description of how the project supports corporate objectives, expressed (if possible) in measurable units.
  - The reasons this project was chosen instead of other alternatives.
- Customer's quality expectations.
- Acceptance Criteria: the requirements that the client sets for the end product.
- Known risks: an inventory of the risks that could threaten the project.
- Outline Project Plan: an initial indication of the costs, lifecycle and delivery date.

Defining Project Approach (SU5)

Before any planning can be done in the initiation stage, it must be determined how the project outcome is to be developed. Is it largely bought in or is the work developed in-house or contracted out? Will it be based on existing products or will completely new products be developed? Etc.

The Project Approach, also called the project strategy, is determined based on the Project Brief, the defined risks in the Risk Log, business and industrial standards and best practice.

Planning an Initiation Stage (SU6)

The Project Initiation Document (PID) and the Stage Plan for the first stage of execution are produced in the initiation stage. The PID forms the basis for the management and execution of the project. Based on the PID and the Stage Plan for the first execution stage, the Project Board can decide whether the project can be started.

The initiation stage is an extremely important stage for the project and obligatory within the PRINCE2 method. Setting up the documents in the initiation stage takes time and money and demands the commitment of people and resources, not only from the client's organisation but also from those who finally must work on the project. The amount of detail in the various documents delivered in the initiation stage must also be determined. Like each Stage Plan, the

Initiation Stage Plan must be detailed, with firm indications of who, what, when and how the project is to be developed. If this is determined only after the initiation stage has been authorised by the Project Board, it will be too late. It will then become apparent that the time required by the persons involved is more than expected and does not agree with the individual work planning. The commitment of various people must again be authorised leading to the first delays.

The Initiation Stage is set up based on what is given in the Project Brief, the risks defined in the Risk Log and the Project Approach.

3.2.4 Input and output

Table 1 gives the input and output of all the subprocesses of the process Starting Up a Project.

Starting Up a Project (SU)

Input	Subprocess	Output
• Project Mandate	SU1 Appointing an Executive and Project Manager	• Project Mandate (update) • Job description: Executive + Project Manager • Appointment of Executive + Project Manager
• Project Mandate (update) • Job description Executive + Project Manager	SU2 Designing a Project Management Team	• Project Management Team Structure • Draft job descriptions of other Project Management Team members
• Project Management Team Structure • Draft job descriptions	SU3 Appointing a Project Management Team	• Appointment of Project Management Team • Definitive job descriptions
• Project Mandate	SU4 Preparing a Project Brief	• Project Brief • Risk Log
• Project Brief • Risk Log	SU5 Defining Project Approach	• Project Approach
• Project Approach • Project Brief • Risk Log	SU6 Planning an Initiation Stage	• Draft Initiation Stage Plan • Risk Log (update)

Table 1 Input and output SU

3.2.5 Responsibilities

Corporate or programme management is responsible for appointing the Executive and the Project Manager. Both in turn are responsible for the composition of the Project Management Team and the job descriptions. The Executive is specifically responsible for the composition of the Project Board, appointing the other people within the Project Management Team and bringing in line with corporate or programme management's objectives, based on proposals made by the Project Manager.

The Executive is responsible for the development of the Project Brief. However, the Project Brief is compiled by the Project manager.

The Project Manager is responsible for setting up the Project Approach and the Initiation Stage Plan. The Project Manager is supported in this by Project Support and Project Assurance, under the supervision of the Senior Supplier. The person responsible for Project Assurance from the Executive must thereby indicate how the Business Case and the risk assessment is to take place.

3.3 Initiating a Project (IP)

3.3.1 Context

IP starts once the Project Board has approved the Project Brief and the other documents of the process Starting Up a Project. This approval is given in the subprocess Authorising Initiation (DP1).

The process Initiating a Project is the second process in the process model. It is, however, the first process in the project. The first process in the process model is the process Starting Up a Project, but this process takes place before the actual start of the project. The process Initiating a Project takes place in the initiation stage and is the most important process in this stage. The process Initiating a Project directs the process Planning (PL) and the process Managing Stage Boundaries (SB).

The process Initiating a Project delivers the Project Initiation Document (PID) and the Stage Plan for the first stage of execution. In the subprocess Authorising a Project (DP2) the Project Board approves these documents and authorises (the first stage of) the work.

The process Initiating a Project starts with assembling the Project Quality Plan. In addition, the Quality Log is set up (IP1). Subsequently, based on the Project Quality Plan and the content of the Project Brief, the Project Plan is set up (IP2). The Business Case is checked and further refined. At the same time, the risks are re-assessed and the Risk Log updated (IP3). Following this, the project controls are set, the Communication Plan is created (IP4) and the Project Files set up (IP5). Finally, the PID is assembled and the Stage Plan for the (first) execution stage set up (IP6). The activities follow a logical sequence, but can also in part be repetitive (see figure 3.4).

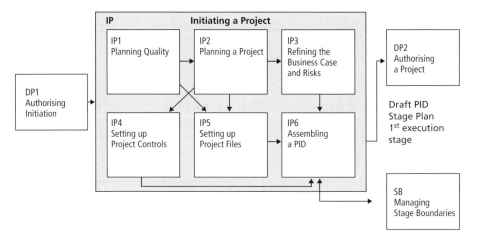

Figure 3.4 Initiating a Project (Based on: OGC source)

3.3.2 Fundamental principles

For a successful project the following applies:
- A project is a finite process with a defined start and end.
- All parties must be clear on the aims of the project, why it is needed, how the outcome is to be achieved and what the responsibilities are of all the parties involved. This creates a support-base.
- Well-managed projects have an increased chance of success.

Problems will occur if there is no clear start and end to the project. Nobody knows where the responsibility for the project ends and where the line organisation starts and vice versa. This leads to mistakes and frustrations and does not benefit the project. Both the start and the end of a project must be clear and well-defined. The process Starting Up a Project defines the project outlines. In the process Initiating a Project, this information is further refined into the Project Initiation Document.

A support-base is one of the most important preconditions for achieving a successful project. This must be worked on from the start of the project. To achieve this, transparency is required, why and by whom and how it is to be achieved.

The basic rule for good project management: 'first think then act' must be followed to ensure a successful project. A comprehensive document for the whole project is required, before the project can be started.

3.3.3 Process description

The purpose of the process Initiating a Project is to ensure that a basic contract is drawn up for the complete project, in the form of a Project Initiation Document. A Stage Plan must also be created for the (first) execution stage giving detailed agreements about who, what, when and how this is to be achieved.

This basic contract and Stage Plan can be formally or informally agreed. However, it is recommended that the basic contract be agreed in writing. Experience has taught that in the weeks and sometimes days following, what is remembered of the verbal agreement between the various parties differs tremendously, particularly if in the meantime the circumstances have changed.

The objectives of the process Initiating a Project are:
- Document and confirm the Business Case for the project.
- Ensure a firm and accepted foundation for the project, prior to commencing work.
- Acquire the 'commitment' of all parties.
- Ensure that the Project Board takes ownership of the project. It is important that the Project Manager keeps in regular contact with the various Project Board members and with the Project Board as a whole to ensure that the PID is a Project Board and Project Manager document and not only the Project Manager's. The more Project Board members take ownership of the project the more support there will be during the project.
- Ensure that the Project Board can make a decision based on the PID as to whether the project is viable (no go/go) and authorise the commitment of people and resources for the first execution stage of the project based on the Stage Plan.
- Provision of an authorised basic document that forms the basis for decision-making during the life of the project.
- Ensure that the initiation stage is carried out in an effective and organised manner.

Planning Quality (IP1)

The objective of this subprocess is to determine the project quality requirements and quality approach. The quality requirements and quality approach are laid down in the Project Quality Plan. This plan includes:
- The quality expectations of the customer for the deliverables.
- The Acceptance Criteria.
- The quality management system for the project.
- The quality assurance for the project.
- The names of those responsible for setting up and managing the quality system.
- The quality assessment techniques and procedures.
- The Configuration Management Plan.
- The procedure for the control of changes.

The customer quality expectations and Acceptance Criteria together form the quality requirements for the project. These are also called 'the basic project requirements'. When determining the quality system for the project, it is recommended that use is made of the customer's and supplier's quality systems (if that is possible). One or more people from the customer and/or supplier can be made specifically responsible for the project's quality assurance.

The Quality Log is created for the project as part of the quality system. All planned quality assessments and the final results are recorded in the Quality Log during the life of the project.

Part of the Configuration Management Plan is setting up the structure of the project documentation. This structure, however, depends upon the Project Plan and the controls to be agreed. In view of the fact that the Project Plan (IP2) and the Controls (IP4) still have to be defined, it is recommended that filling in of the project documentation structure be shifted to a later initiation stage. The subprocess Setting up Project Files (IP5) provides for this.

The subprocess Planning Quality makes use of the Project Brief, the Project Approach and the customer's and supplier's quality standards. The output of the subprocess is the Project Quality Plan and the Quality Log.

Planning a Project (IP2)

The Project Plan is an outline plan for the complete execution stage of the project.
The Project Plan gives:

- The most important activities.
- The deliverables.
- The costs.
- The lifecycle.
- Required commitment of people and resources.

The Project Plan must be determined before any costs are incurred by the project. The Project Plan gives the input for the Business Case and forms an important part of the PID. When producing the Project Plan, use is made of the process Planning and the risks are again updated.

If the Project Manager expects that a lot of changes will be implemented during the project, the Project Manager can propose to the Project Board that a separate budget be included for a Request for a Change. This avoids the Executive returning to corporate or programme management during the course of the project for an additional budget.

The subprocess Planning a Project makes use of the Project Brief, the Project Approach and the Project Quality Plan. The Project Plan is setup and the Risk Log updated.

Refining the Business Case and Risks (IP3)

The Business Case describes why a project needs to be done and how the project meets the customer's corporate objectives. In addition, the Business Case describes the trade off between the costs, benefits and risks that come with the project. During the project the Business Case must be updated as soon as important decisions need to be taken.

The Business Case is compiled before the start of the project by the corporate or programme management and forms the basis for the Project Mandate. During the process Starting Up a Project, the Project Manager checks whether there is a Business Case and takes the main points included in the Business Case over to the Project Brief. During the subprocess IP3, the Business Case is refined. The main points upon which the Business Case was based must be checked to see whether they are still valid:

- Are the benefits the customer expects to achieve from the deliverables still correct?
- Are any new benefits expected or have certain benefits disappeared?
- Are the estimated costs and duration times correct and if not what will the consequences be for the Business Case?
- What are the risks and do the risks indicate that the Project Approach or the Project Plan and therefore the Business Case should be adapted?

Sometimes the Project Quality Plan must be adapted and, for example, the quality requirements adjusted in order to be able to achieve a positive Business Case.

For the subprocess Refining the Business Case and Risks use is made of the Project Brief, the Project Approach, the Project Plan and the Risk Log. The output of the subprocess is a refined Business Case. The Risk Log is updated and, if necessary, the Project Plan reworked.

Setting up Project Controls (IP4)

Each decision on the project has to be made in a timely and well-considered manner. This is possible only if the decision-makers are provided with the information in time. Monitoring mechanisms must ensure that for every level of the Project Management Team the next level can:

- Check the progress.
- Compare the progress with the plan.
- Check plans and options based on various scenarios.
- Trace problems.
- Take corrective measures and authorise future activities.

A Communication Plan must be created in order to determine what information should be provided, by whom, to whom, how and when. As soon as the first three subprocesses of IP have been completed and the structure and cohesion of the relevant documents determined, the project controls and communication lines can be determined. The monitoring mechanisms and communication lines to be agreed depend, among other things, upon the duration time, complexity, risks, stakeholders involved and the question of whether the project is critical or not. The controls and communication lines must therefore also be specifically defined per project. In this use can be made of the controls overview given in chapter 4.

The subprocess Setting up Project Controls makes use of the Project Quality Plan, the Project Plan and the Risk Log. The Project Plan and the Risk Log are adapted if necessary. The output of the subprocess is the controls to be applied and the Communication Plan.

Setting up Project Files (IP5)

Once the project is underway, the project information must be managed. The project information is the most important 'business asset' of the project. The manner in which company information is managed has been laid down in the Configuration Management Plan in the subprocess IP1. The actual setting up of the project filing structure depends upon the Project Plan and the agreed project controls, and can now be done.

The subprocess Setting up Project Files makes use of the Project Plan. The output of the subprocess is the project filing structure. With this the Configuration Management Plan is completed as part of the Project Quality Plan. Furthermore, the Issue Log, Lessons Learned Log and Daily Log are created.

Assembling a Project Initiation Document (IP6)

One basic document is needed containing all information relevant to the project. This is the Project Initiation Document (PID). This document is necessary in order to gain authorisation for the project and serves as the basic document for the project itself.

The PID is compiled based on all information produced up to this point. The PID is, however, not an amalgamation of all previous documents but a management document for decision-making by the Project Board. For larger projects it is recommended that the actual documents from all the previous processes be included in an appendix or referred to and included as a separate text of the main points in the actual PID. This is done to prevent the PID from becoming too bulky a document.

The Project Board cannot approve the start of the first execution stage simply on the basis of the PID. Besides the PID, a detailed plan for the first execution stage is necessary. From the subprocess IP6, the process Managing Stage Boundaries (SB) is invoked in which the Stage Plan for the first execution stage is prepared.

The Stage Plan for the first execution stage is not included in the PID. The PID and the Stage Plan remain separate documents. The PID is often sent for validation to the corporate or programme management by the Project Board. The Stage Plan is assessed by the Project Board only.

The subprocess Assembling a Project Initiation Document makes use of all the documents that have been compiled in SU and IP prior to IP6. The subprocess IP6 triggers the process Managing Stage Boundaries. The output of the subprocess is the draft PID and the Stage Plan for the first execution stage.

3.3.4 Input and output

Table 2 gives the input and output of all the subprocesses of the process Initiating a Project.

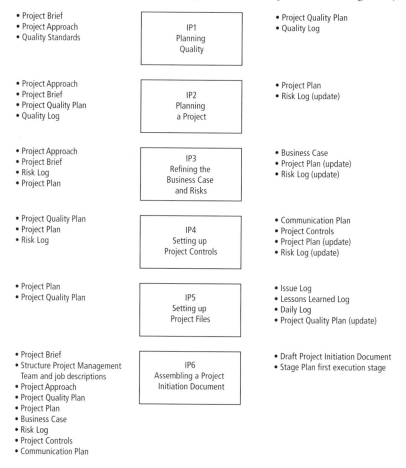

Input	Process	Output
• Project Brief • Project Approach • Quality Standards	IP1 Planning Quality	• Project Quality Plan • Quality Log
• Project Approach • Project Brief • Project Quality Plan • Quality Log	IP2 Planning a Project	• Project Plan • Risk Log (update)
• Project Approach • Project Brief • Risk Log • Project Plan	IP3 Refining the Business Case and Risks	• Business Case • Project Plan (update) • Risk Log (update)
• Project Quality Plan • Project Plan • Risk Log	IP4 Setting up Project Controls	• Communication Plan • Project Controls • Project Plan (update) • Risk Log (update)
• Project Plan • Project Quality Plan	IP5 Setting up Project Files	• Issue Log • Lessons Learned Log • Daily Log • Project Quality Plan (update)
• Project Brief • Structure Project Management Team and job descriptions • Project Approach • Project Quality Plan • Project Plan • Business Case • Risk Log • Project Controls • Communication Plan	IP6 Assembling a Project Initiation Document	• Draft Project Initiation Document • Stage Plan first execution stage

Table 2 Input and output IP

3.3.5 Responsibilities

The Project Manager is responsible for the process Initiating a Project. The Project Manager may be supported by Project Support and specialists during the stages of the project. The Project Manager can also contract out parts in Work Packages to third parties. The Project Manager receives advice from those responsible for Project Assurance. The Project Manager aligns the content of his activities to the aims of the Project Board and other stakeholders directly involved. At the end of the process the Project Board members and the Project Manager both have ownership of the process result.

3.4 Directing a Project (DP)

3.4.1 Context

This process runs throughout the project. The process starts directly after the process Starting Up a Project and continues until project closure and includes:

- Authorising the initiation stage.
- Project direction and control.
- Liaising with corporate or programme management.
- Confirming project closure.

The process Directing a Project starts with the authorisation of the initiation stage, based on the documents provided from the process Starting Up a Project. Based on the Project Initiation Document and the Stage Plan for the first execution stage the project is authorised and the start approved for the first execution stage. During the project's life cycle the Project Board makes the decisions about the progress (no go/go) based on the Stage or Exception Plans. During the various stages, the Project Board gives ad hoc direction to the Project Manager. Finally, the Project Board confirms project closure to the stakeholder parties (see figure 3.5).

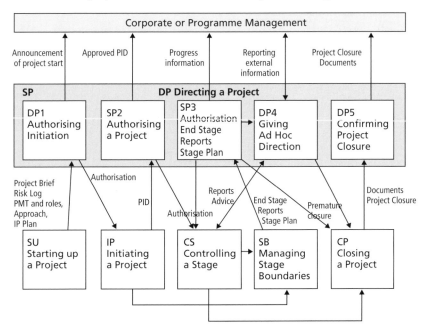

Figure 3.5 Directing a Project (Based on: OGC source)

3.4.2 Fundamental principles

The Project Board is responsible for the project and must have authority in order to:
- Determine the project outcome.
- Make funds available for the project.
- Guarantee commitment of people and resources.
- Take care of the communication lines to external stakeholders.

The process Directing a Project does not encompass the Project Manager's day-to-day management of the project but the Project Board's overall management of the project. The basis here is 'management by exception'. The Project Board directs the project via a relatively small number of decision points. Regular progress meetings are not necessary. In the meantime, the Project Manager informs the Project Board by way of the Highlight Report and informs the Project Board of any exceptions to the agreed plan if the previously agreed tolerance limits are threatened.

Communication to corporate or programme management and other external interested parties is laid down in the Communication Plan.

3.4.3 Process description

The objective of the process Directing a Project is to guarantee project success. This takes place by ensuring that the agreed outcome is delivered within the agreed time, costs and quality parameters, so that corporate or programme management is able to achieve the benefits included in the Business Case. The assumption is that a project is successful if all the stakeholder parties are satisfied with the result at the end of the project.
The Project Board activities are:
- Ensure effective day-to-day management of the people and resources concerned.
- Guarantee the required commitment of people and resources.
- Give 'overall' direction to the project.
- Manage the identified risks.
- Make decisions on any changes and other Project Issues.
- Make decisions where tolerances threaten to be exceeded.
- Ensure that the deliverables are consistent with corporate or management objectives.
- Ensure that the necessary communication and reporting lines within the project are in place.
- Support the necessary external communication and publicity.

Authorising Initiation (DP1)

Before a start can be made with the initiation stage, the Project Board must determine:
- What the project content is.
- That it is right to start with the project.
- What the initial activities will encompass.

The subprocess Authorising Initiation is the first subprocess of the process Directing a Project. The Project Board must decide whether authorisation can be given for the initiation stage. The Project Board must furthermore:
- Formally confirm the members of the Project Management Team and approve the job descriptions.
- Approve the Project Brief and have it ratified by corporate or programme management.
- Approve the Project Approach.
- Approve the Initiation Stage Plan.

- Guarantee the required commitment of people and resources based upon this plan.
- Inform the organisation hosting the project of the project start.

The subprocess Authorising Initiation makes use of the Project Brief from the process Starting Up a Project. The output of the subprocess is the formal approval of these documents, as well as the authorisation of the project start to the Project Manager and the announcement of the project start to the host organisation.

Authorising a Project (DP2)

The costs of a project are often considerable. Before the actual project can start there must therefore be:
- An acceptable Business Case for the project.
- A check on whether it meets relevant corporate or programme management strategy.
- An accurate estimate of the duration times and costs involved in the complete project and the required budget released.
- An assessment and acceptance of the risks of the project.
- A check on whether the project will be appropriately controlled.

In the subprocess Authorising a Project, the PID is approved and the project authorised. The Project Board brings the PID in alignment with corporate or programme management strategy. If there is not a good Business Case for the project, the Project Board will not authorise the project and the project will be stopped (no go).

This subprocess makes use of the draft Project Initiation Document that is created during the process Initiating a Project. It delivers the formal approval of the PID and gives authorisation for the project. The start of the project can, however, only be released if the initiation stage has also been correctly closed and the Stage Plan for the first execution stage approved. Parallel and in conjunction with this, the subprocess Authorising a Project (DP2), the subprocess Authorising a Stage or Exception Plan (DP3) will be also carried out at the end of the initiation stage.

Authorising a Stage or Exception Plan (DP3)

It is important that work commences on a stage only once the Project Board has given its explicit permission. In order to make this possible, the project must be broken down into manageable sections (stages). At the end of each stage the Project Board has to approve whether the project's activities are to continue or not. This also provides the opportunity of tracing problems early on in the project and of reacting accordingly.

If the Project Board gives its approval, it is obliged to release the required commitment of people and resources. The Project Board bases these decisions on:
- The actual status of the project and an account of the previous stage.
- The Stage Plan of the next stage with a detailed plan of the commitment of people and resources required, and the deliverables.
- An up-to-date assessment of the remaining part of the Project Plan.
- A reassessment of the risks.
- An up-to-date assessment of the Business Case and the benefits to be achieved.

This subprocess can also be invoked if the Project Manager sees that, during the stage, a stage tolerance will be exceeded and based on an earlier decision of the Project Board the Project Manager has created an Exception Plan (SB6).

With the Stage Plan, the stage tolerances are also agreed for the next stage. The stage tolerances for the various stages are laid down in the PID and, in principle, do not need to be reassessed, except if there is reason to do so.

If the project tolerances threaten to be exceeded, the Project Board must bring them back in line with the corporate or programme management requirements. During this process, the Project Board also informs the stakeholders of the project's progress, in agreement with that which is laid down in the Communication Plan.

In this process, the Project Board must guarantee that changes in the (business) environment of the project are known to the Project Manager and that the Project Manager has anticipated this in the plans. The subprocess Authorising a Stage or Exception Plan is the time to confirm changes to the Project Management Team, if required.

This subprocess makes use of the documents created or updated by the Project manager from the subprocess Managing Stage Boundaries. When making decisions, the Project Board falls back on the existing PID and the Stage Plan for the current stage. The output of the subprocess is the approved Stage and Exception Plan, the authorisation of the next stage or the instruction to prematurely close the project. In this process, information on progress is also released for the stakeholders.

If the project is no longer viable, the Project Board will instruct the Project Manager to terminate the project prematurely. The Project Manager will then trigger the process Closing a Project (CP).

Giving Ad Hoc Direction (DP4)

Even when a stage is proceeding according to plan, it may be necessary for the Project Manager and Project Board members to make readjustments in line with each other. Examples are:
• Directions to the Project Board as a result of external events.
• Solving problems concerning commitment of people and resources.
• Solving conflicts between parties.
• Decision-making as a result of the Project Manager requesting advice.
• Changes in the composition of the Project Board members.

The Project Manager must inform the Project Board about progress, as well as if work is not going completely to plan. No news is not automatically good news. The Project Board members must (as project owners) be informed of the progress and ensure that the project goes to plan. The Project Manager informs the Project Board at previously agreed intervals with a Highlight Report about progress, the Project Issues and the risk status. Both internal and external events can trigger the subprocess Giving Ad Hoc Direction.

The Project Board makes decisions concerning Request for Changes falling outside the Project Manager's responsibility, such as indications of products already approved. This is done on the basis of 'request for advice' from the Project Manager. The Project Board must also make the required people and resources available in order to carry out an approved Request for Change. In this process, as with DP3, the Project Board informs the stakeholders of the progress as laid down in the Communication Plan.

If during a stage there is a threat of the stage tolerances being exceeded, the Project Manager seeks to bring this attention point as a Project Issue to the Project Board via an Exception Report

(CS8). Based on this report, the Project Board determines whether the project should continue or not and if so, how the remaining part of the stage must be finished. If necessary, the Project Manager initiates the process Managing Stage Boundaries (SB) based upon the decision of the Project Board and creates an Exception Plan.

If the project threatens to fall outside the stage tolerances and/or if the project threatens to deviate from what was agreed in the Project Brief, the Project Board puts this to the corporate or programme management.

If the project is no longer viable, the Project Board, as with the process DP3, will instruct the Project Manager to prematurely close the project. The Project Manager will then trigger the process Closing a Project (CP).

The Highlight Report, the Exception Report, request for advice and external information provide the input of this subprocess. In this subprocess, the Project Board puts together the Checkpoint Reports for corporate or programme management, gives them advice and gives orders to the Project Manager. In this subprocess, the Project Board makes use of what is laid down in the PID and the current Stage Plan.

Confirming Project Closure (DP5)

In order for a project to close, the Project Board must ensure that:
- A service and support organisation is set up for the deliverables.
- The project has a clearly defined end and that the project outcome is formally handed over to those responsible for service and support.
- Responsibility and ownership of the deliverables are formally handed over to the end users.
- The people and resources are released for their individual organisations.
- Any outstanding action points and lessons learned from the project are directed to the relevant business sections.
- A plan is set up in order to measure the estimated benefits.
- A recommendation for closure of the project is given to corporate or programme management.
- The Project Manager is discharged.

The subprocess Confirming Project Closure is triggered by the Project Manager from the process Closing a Project. The subprocess Confirming Project Closure comprises initiating the final activities of the Project Board for the project. In this subprocess the Project Board also informs the stakeholders about the closure of the project.

This subprocess makes use of the documents that are delivered in the process Closing a Project. The output of this subprocess is the Recommendation for Closing a Project from the Project Board to corporate or programme management. In this subprocess, the Project Board makes use of what is laid down in the PID and the Communication Plan.

3.4.4 Input and output

Table 3 gives the input and output of all subprocesses of the process Directing a Project.

Directing a Project (DP)

Input	Subprocess	Output
• Project Management Team Structure and job descriptions • Project Brief • Risk Log • Project Approach • Draft Initiation Stage Plan	**DP1** Authorising Initiation	• Project Brief • Initiation Stage Plan • Announcement of project start • Authorisation of initiation
• Draft Project Initiation Document • Stage Plan 1st execution stage	**DP2** Authorising a Project	• Project Initiation Document • Approved Stage Plan • Project Authorisation
• Next stage Plan/Exception Plan • Project Plan • Business Case • Project Initiation Document • Changes to the Project Management Team • Risk Log • End Stage Report • Request for authorisation to proceed	**DP3** Authorising a Stage or Exception Plan	• Approved Stage Plan/Exception Plan • Authorisation to proceed to the next stage • Progress information to third parties in accordance with the Communication Plan • Decision for premature closure
• Highlight Report • Exception Report • Request for advice • Communication Plan • Information from external sources	**DP4** Giving Ad Hoc Direction	• Reporting to Corporate or Programme Management • Advice from the Project Group • Request to setup Exception Plan • Decision for premature closure
• Acceptance delivery end users • Acceptance delivery by maintenance and control • End Project Report • Follow-on Action Recommendations • Post-Project Review Plan • Lessons Learned Report • Project Initiation Document • Communication Plan	**DP5** Confirming Project Closure	• End Project Report • Follow-on Action Recommendations • Post-Project Review Plan • Lessons Learned Report • Announcement of Project Closure

Table 3 Input and output DP

3.4.5 Responsibilities

The Project Board is responsible for the process Directing a Project. The information required in the process is supplied primarily by the Project Manager. The Project Board gets other information from external sources. The Project Board may be supported with the various subprocesses by those who are responsible for Project Assurance (if this responsibility is delegated to third parties).

The final decision for approval of the Project Brief and later the Project Initiation Document lies with corporate or programme management. Possible deviations from what is laid down in the Project Brief and the Business Case must be put to corporate or programme management by the Project Board for approval. Any possibility that project tolerances will be exceeded must also be brought to the attention of corporate or programme management by the Project Board.

Corporate or programme management also decide the communication lines with various external project stakeholders. The Project Board is responsible within the Project Management Team for providing the given guidelines. A large proportion of intrinsic communication activities are often taken care of by the Project Manager.

3.5 Controlling a Stage (CS)

3.5.1 Context
The process Controlling a Stage starts once the Project Board has approved the Stage Plan of the stage involved and approved release of the work involved in the subprocess Authorising a Stage or Exception Plan (DP3). The subprocess DP3 triggers the subprocess Authorising Work Packages (CS1) for the release of the initial Work Package in the stage concerned.

In the process Controlling a Stage, the Project Manager directs the Team Manager, whose activities are described in the process Managing a Product Delivery. The interfaces between both main processes are Authorising Work Packages (CS1), Assessing Progress (CS2) and Receiving Completed Work Package (CS9).

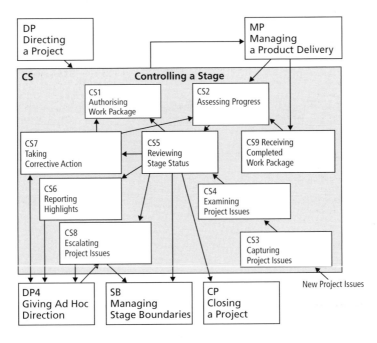

Figure 3.6 Controlling a Stage (Based on: OGC source)

The Project Manager reports periodically to the Project Board by means of a Highlight Report (CS6). Furthermore, the Project Board gives ad hoc direction from DP4 to the Project Manager, such as:
• The Project Manager asks the Project Board for advice and to make interim decisions, for example approval of corrective action, perhaps as a result of a Request for Change, in CS7.
• The Highlight Report and/or internal and external events and initiatives provide a reason for the Project Board to pass on advice and/or decisions to the Project Manager. Based on this,

the Project Manager undertakes the necessary activities in CS7.
- Where the stage tolerance is expected to be exceeded, the Project Manager escalates Project Issues to the Project Board by means of an Exception Report in CS8.

From Reviewing Stage Status (CS5) the Programme Manager triggers the processes Managing Stage Boundaries (SB) and Closing a Project (CP). In the event of an escalation the process Managing Stage Boundaries is triggered from Escalating Project Issues (CS8) (see figure 3.6).

3.5.2 Fundamental principles

This process describes the Project Manager's day-to-day management during the various stages of the project (see figure 3.7).

As soon as a decision is taken to carry out the work of a stage and the commitment of people and resources is released, the Project Management Team must direct itself at the delivery of the agreed products and services:
- In agreement with defined quality requirements.
- Within the agreed costs, commitment of people and resources and time planning, in order to ensure that finally the defined benefits (after project closure) can be achieved.

Figure 3.7 Command circle Controlling a Stage

In order to achieve this within a stage, project management must be directed at:
- The delivery of the agreed stage products.
- The efficient and effective commitment of the required people and resources.
- Controlling risks.
- Keeping an eye on the agreed Business Case (also the benefits).
- Keeping an eye on every possible change to the agreed scope and products, in order to prevent uncontrolled changes occurring.

If changes are required by the parties, then the consequences of these changes must be thoroughly investigated by the Project Manager and the Project Board must subsequently authorise these changes.

3.5.3 Process description

Authorising a Work Package (CS1)
Work can begin only if the Project Manager has made explicit agreements with the Team Manager responsible. To instruct the Team Manager properly it is necessary to have clear agreements on what must be achieved, the estimated costs, commitment of people and resources, the time to completion, quality aspects, relationship with other products and interim reporting arrangements.

A Product Description must be set up of all the deliverables including a product description, the product components, which documents and products must be used from third parties to achieve this, what quality requirements are set for the product, how the product is to be tested for these requirements and by whom.

When authorising a Work Package the Project Manager must further ensure that:
• There are sufficient people and resources available to carry out the work.
• The Team Manager is aware of the project quality procedures, particularly regarding management of change and configuration management.
• Specific problems and risks are identified and the necessary actions taken against them.
• The Team Manager has ownership (and considers himself owner!) of the Work Package.

The Project Manager must pay careful attention to the Work Package. The Project Manager must discuss the handing over of the Work Package with the Team Manager. Often it becomes apparent that small changes to what was previously agreed in the Stage Plan are needed because in the meantime the situation has changed and it becomes necessary to manage new problems and risk. The Project Manager must adapt the Stage Plan to this eventuality (within the tolerances; otherwise the Project Manager must escalate the problems to the Project Board). These minor changes also ensure that the Team Manager will also be made to feel owner of the Work Package.

The counterpart activities of the Team Manager in this subprocess are described in the subprocess Work Package (MP1).

A condition for handing-over the Work Package to the Team Manager is that the Team Manager has sufficient expertise and authority to be able to carry responsibility of the Work Package. If this is not the case, a different Team Manager must be sought, or the Project Manager must fulfil the role of Team Manager and directly allocate individual activities of the Work Package to the various team members. This is only recommended for smaller projects and if the Project Manager has sufficient expertise for the Work Package concerned. In larger and more complex projects, this is not the best solution. The Project Manager is often so consumed by the activities of Team Manager that his own work as Project Manager comes under threat. This must be avoided.

The input for this subprocess is the Authorisation to proceed with the Stage or Exception Plan including the relevant Product Descriptions and information from the subprocess Taking Corrective Action (CS7). Following the hand-over meeting with the Team manager, it may be necessary to update the Work Package, the Stage or Exception Plan and the Risk Log. The configuration management database must also be updated. The output of this subprocess is the formal hand-over of the Work Package to the Team Manager.

Assessing Progress (CS2)

In order to manage the project, the Project Manager must know what the status of the work is in relation to the plan. It is possible that 'fire-fighting' by the Project Manager may dominate a stage resulting in participants losing sight of the overall goal. Good assessment of progress makes sure that the focus stays on the deliverables in this stage.

The Project Manager collects the necessary information for assessing the progress from progress meetings. The Team Managers reports the progress using Checkpoint Reports. Furthermore, the Project Manager bases his information on entries in the Quality Log, configuration management database and information from Receiving Completed Work Packages (CS9).

Reporting about the progress includes:
- Progress information of the work.
- Costs and commitment of people and resources.
- The products delivered.
- The time still to be spent, costs to be made and required commitment of people and resources.
- Attention points important for the progress of the stage.

Using this information the Stage Plan is updated.

The Project Manager is responsible for monitoring progress. The Project Manager is usually assisted in this by Project Support. If there is a separate Configuration Librarian, then the 'configuration status report' is provided by the Configuration Librarian with an update of the configuration management database.

Capturing Project Issues (CS3)

Problems, attention points and changes can occur at any time during the project. These are called Project Issues. These Project Issues must be recorded. Everyone involved in the project can raise Project Issues.

Project Issues must not be forgotten, even when there is no immediate solution or when not immediately acted upon. If Project Managers of projects that have run into big problems are asked, almost all of them will admit that there were advance indications of problems. But because nothing could be done with them at that particular moment, the problems were put aside and picked up again too late.

Capturing Project Issues normally takes place ad hoc. The Project Issues are identified and recorded in the Issue Log.

Project Issues can be subdivided into:
- A Request for Change.
- An Off-Specification.
- Other Project Issues.

The various types of Project Issues are described in the PRINCE2 component Change Control. Different procedures can be agreed per Project Issue type. Possible procedures are discussed in the technique Change control approach.

As soon as a Project Issue is recorded, a preliminary examination of its impact must be carried out. Based on this, a preliminary priority is determined. The person who has triggered the Project Issue is informed that the Project Issue has been recorded and included in the Issue procedure.

The Project Manager is responsible for capturing Project Issues. Project Support or the Configuration Librarian is usually responsible for the entering of various Project Issues and dealing with them.

The output of the subprocess is the result of the initial examination of the Project Issue and, in addition, the Issue Log is updated.

Examining Project Issues (CS4)

Before deciding on a course of action as a result of a Project Issue, the impact of the Project Issue must first be examined by the Project Manager.

Additionally, all Project Issues that have yet to be dealt with must be examined periodically and a course of action defined for the decision-making during the process Reviewing Stage Status (CS5). A decision about a Project Issue can only be taken within the framework of a general assessment of the status of the project. Very urgent Project Issues are the exception here.

Project Issues that must be dealt with within the framework of a programme must be closed within the project and handed-over to the programme by the Project Board.

Examining Project Issues covers:
• Assembling all relevant information and determining the consequences for the project (timescales, costs, commitment of people and resources, risks, results and benefits to be delivered).
• Updating the Risk Log.
• Formulating recommendations.

The Project Manager is responsible for this subprocess. Assessment can be done by third parties. The administrative work may be delegated to Project Support. The Configuration Librarian is responsible for maintaining the Issue Log. The request for change must be approved by the Project Board or by the designated Change Authority.

When assessing the Project Issues use is made of the Stage Plan, the Project Plan and the Business Case. The Issue Log and (if applicable) the Risk Log are updated.

Reviewing Stage Status (CS5)

If during a project the status is not checked regularly, it will almost certainly get out of control. Checking the status of the project against the plan can prevent this. Further it must be decided whether:
• The subsequent Work Packages should be started.
• The Stage or Exception Plan must be modified.

The stage status must be checked based on the information from the subprocess Assessing Progress (CS2) and the results from subprocess Examining Project Issues (CS4).

The activities in Reviewing Stage Status cover:
- Reviewing the work progress in relation to the Stage Plan.
- Reviewing the effect of Project Issues and of the decisions proposed in relation to the Stage Plan, Project Plan and Business Case, and of the Request for Change in relation to the change budget (if present).
- Establishing whether work in the stage will remain within the tolerances.
- Checking that the Business Case is still valid.
- Checking whether new risks have arisen and/or whether existing risks have changed.
- Deciding whether new work needs to be started (via CS1).
- Deciding whether corrective action needs to be taken (via CS7).
- Deciding whether advice is needed from the Project Board, for example, decision making on corrective action associated with a Request for Change (via CS7).
- Deciding whether to escalate Project Issues to the Project Board (via CS8) if it is expected that the agreed tolerances in a stage are to be exceeded.
- Triggering the process Managing Stage Boundaries or the process Closing a Project if it becomes apparent that the stage (or project) is coming to an end.

The Project Manager is responsible for reviewing the status of the stage. The Project Manager may be supported by Project Support, the Configuration Librarian, the person(s) responsible for Project Assurance and if required, by the Project Board members.

When reviewing the status of a stage the Project Manager uses the updated Stage Plan, Project Plan, Business Case and the configuration management database. The output of the subprocess is information about the status of the stage and leads to decision-making on project modifications, or the closing of the stage or closing of a project, and triggers the agreed (sub)processes.

The Daily Log is often used by the Project Manager to register lots of small activities.

Reporting Highlights (CS6)
The Project Board has overall responsibility for the project. The Project Manager is responsible for the day-to-day management of the project. Good reporting from the Project Manager to the Project Board and the stakeholders keeps the Project Board and stakeholders informed and involved in the project and the Project Board is put in the position of exercising its responsibility.

The Project Manager periodically informs the Project Board using the Highlight Report. The frequency of the Highlight Report is laid down in the process IP4 and in the PID. The Communication Plan (also part of the PID) indicates which stakeholders are to be informed, when and the information to be given.

In subprocess CS6, the Project Manager makes use of the updated Stage Plan, Communication Plan, Risk Log, Issue Log, and the Quality Log. The Project Manager collects all the necessary information, writes it in the Highlight Report with other progress information such as that agreed in the Communication Plan and distributes it to those concerned.

Taking Corrective Action (CS7)
Adjustments and changes to a project need to be carried out in a structured manner.
Adjustments are triggered from the subprocess Reviewing Stage Status (CS5). It may be necessary to get the advice from Project Board members before corrective action takes place or

from the Change Authority if this responsibility has been delegated. Decisions from the Project Board may also be needed, such as approval or disapproval of the Request for Change. Here the link is to the subprocess Giving Ad Hoc Control (DP4) of the Project Board. This subprocess triggers the corrective actions and the authorisation of the Work Packages (CS1).

The Project Manager collects the necessary information about the change, analyses the effect of the change on the project, compares potential project options and selects the most appropriate option. The Project Manager updates the Stage Plan and if necessary, the relevant Product Descriptions and the configuration management database. The Project Manager makes the necessary information available and finally triggers the corrective action.

Where necessary the Project Manager asks for advice, or a decision from the Project Board. If the corrective action arises from a Project Issue determined earlier, a number of these steps will already have taken place.

When taking correction measures the Project Manager uses (and updates) the Stage Plan, Issue Log, Risk Log and the configuration management database. For recording small corrections, the Project Manager may make use of the Daily Log.

Escalating Project Issues (CS8)

A stage should not go outside the tolerances agreed without approval from the Project Board. Before this threat takes place, the Project Manager must inform the Project Board and advise how to continue.

Setting tolerances is one of the most important controls the Project Board has. Tolerances for timescales and costs, and if necessary, for the scope, quality, risk and benefits must be determined. If the Project Manager expects a tolerance in a stage to be exceeded, this must be escalated by the Project Manager to the Project Board using an Exception Report. The layout of an Exception Report is described further in appendix 7.2.10.

Important causes for exceeding the tolerance margins are Project Issues, as well as bad estimates, people and resources not being made available, poor performance, and unforeseen work and repairs.

The Project Manager analyses the cause, gives the consequences of the changes to the project, describes the possible options and consequences of these options and recommends the option that appears most suitable. With the cause and the options, the consequences for the Stage Plan, Project Plan and risks are investigated, as well as the consequences for the Business Case. Based on what has taken place the Project Manager creates an Exception Report and sends it to the Project Board. It is, of course, recommended that this be discussed with the Project Board in advance.

Based on the Exception Report, the Project Board can decide (in DP4), to remove the cause of the exception, or decide for an alternative course of action. The Project Board can also decide for premature closure of the project. If the Project Board chooses for an alternative course of action they will instruct the Project Manager accordingly. Subsequently from this subprocess the Project Manager triggers the process Managing Stage Boundaries (SB) and the Exception Plan will be set up based upon the option chosen. The Exception Plan covers the remaining section of the current Stage Plan until the new stage boundary.

The Project Manager uses the PID, Stage Plan, Project Plan, Business Case, Issue Log and the Risk Log when escalating Project Issues. The output of the process is a Draft Exception Report for the Project to examine (DP4).

Once the Project Board has examined this, the Project Manager is given the approved Exception Report and instructed to setup an Exception Plan including the approach to be taken. In this subprocess, the configuration management database must also be updated.

Receiving Completed Work Package (CS9)

A formal check of work allocated must be carried out in order to determine whether it has been completed, accepted and handed-over before it can be released to the customer. This also applies to Work Packages allocated to Team Managers.

This subprocess registers the successful delivery of the Work Package, such as handed-over by the Team Manager from MP3. Subsequently this registration is the input for the subprocess Assessing Progress (CS2).

The Project Manager must check that:
- All approvals defined in the quality criteria are in order.
- Those who will use the products have accepted them.
- Everything has been registered in the Quality Log.
- All records have been updated in the configuration management database.
- The products have been transferred to configuration management.

3.5.4 Input and output

Table 4 gives the input and output of all subprocesses in Controlling a Stage.

Input	Subprocess	Output
• Authorisation stage • Work trigger • Product Descriptions • Stage Plan or Exception Plan • Configuration Item Records • Risk Log	**CS1** Authorising Work Package	• Work Package • Stage Plan (update) • Configuration Item Records (update) • Risk Log (update)
• Checkpoint Report • Quality Log • Work Package status	**CS2** Assessing Progress	• Stage Plan (update) • Stage status information
• New Project Issues • Issue Log	**CS3** Capturing Project Issues	• Issue Log (update)
• Issue Log • Risk Log • Business Case • Stage Plan • Project Plan	**CS4** Examining Project Issues	• Issue Log (update) • Risk Log (update)
• Stage status information • Configuration Item Records • Issue & Risk Log • Business Case • Stage Plan & Project Plan	**CS5** Reviewing Stage Status	• Stage status information • Signal to start work • Signal deviation plan deviation • Signal possible tolerance threat • Stage/Project end notification
• Stage status information • Issue & Risk Log • Quality Log • Stage Plan • Communication Plan	**CS6** Reporting Highlights	• Highlight Report • Communication to interested parties
• Plan deviation • Stage Plan • Issue & Risk Log • Configuration Item Records • Project Board guidance	**CS7** Taking Corrective Action	• Signal to start work • Request for advice • Stage Plan (update) • Issue & Risk Log (update) • Configuration Item Records
• Signal possible tolerance threat • PID & Business Case • Stage Plan & Project Plan • Issue & Risk Log • Configuration Item Records	**CS8** Escalating Project Issues	• Exception Report • Configuration Item Records (update) • Exception Plan Request (DP4) • Approved Exception Report
• Approved Work Package • Configuration Item Records	**CS9** Receiving Completed Work Package	• Signed-off Work Package • Configuration database (update)

Table 4 Input and output CS

3.5.5 Responsibilities

The Project Manager is responsible for the process Controlling a Stage. The Project Manager tailors the work to that of the Team Managers. The Project Manager can be assisted in the work by Project Support and by the Configuration Librarian. Project Support monitors the progress and administrative work of all sorts of procedures and reports. The Configuration Librarian updates the Issue Log and the configuration management database. The Configuration Librarian provides the Project Manager with information based on the configuration status report.

The Project Board advises the Project Manager with day-to-day management concerning, among other things, Project Issues and how to deal with changes outside the project. The Project Board makes decisions on a Request for Change. Furthermore, the Project Board instructs the Project Manager as to whether a stage should be brought forward or prematurely closed or even possibly that the project should be prematurely closed.

3.6 Managing Product Delivery (MP)

3.6.1 Context

The process Managing Product Delivery has a direct link with the process Controlling a Stage. The subprocess Accepting a Work Package (MP1) controls the process.

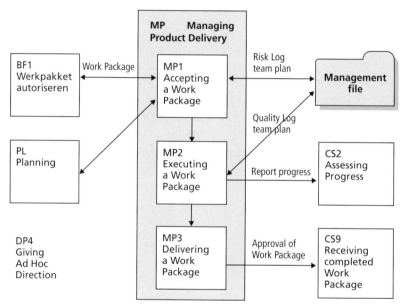

Figure 3.8 Managing Product Delivery

The work described in the process MP can also be carried out without making use of the PRINCE2 methodology. The separate processes CS and MP make a controlled split possible between those who can and those who cannot work with the PRINCE2 method (see figure 3.8).

3.6.2 Fundamental principles

This process allows for a controlled break between the work of the Project Manager and those responsible for the realisation of the deliverables.

The process Managing Product Delivery assumes that the work is divided such that the Project Manager directs work to the Team Manager based on Work Packages. The working relationship between the Project Manager and Team Manager can best be described as a working relationship between the Project Manager and 'preferred supplier'. It does not matter whether the Team

Manager actually has a complete team carrying out the work, or whether the team carrying out the work consists of one person and the Team Manager. Essentially, it is the Project Manager who delegates the responsibility for the Work Package to the Team Manager.

When the team member cannot be responsible for the Work Package, only then the Project Manager is able to delegate tasks and the Project Manager remains responsible for developing the work of the Work Package. The team member then simply remains a team member and the Project Manager in effect fulfils a double role as Project Manager and Team Manager. It is possible that the Project Manager will direct a number of Team Managers for developing the work of different Work Packages, but that for one or more of the Work Packages the Project Manager also fulfils the role of Team Manager.

3.6.3 Process description

The Team Manager's work comprises:
- Accepting a Work Package.
- Executing a Work Package.
- Delivering a Work Package.

Accepting a Work Package (MP1)

Before the work can be started there must be an agreement between the Project Manager and Team Manager about how the work is to be carried out. It is not the case that the Project Manager simply directs the Team Manager to carry the work out. The fact of the matter is that Team Manager is responsible for the technical and practical feasibility of the work to be carried out. The Team Manager is answerable to the Senior Supplier, who on behalf of the supplier has made contract agreements (DP3) with the customer in order to achieve the deliverables.

The Work Package comprises:
- Product Descriptions of the deliverables.
- Interfaces which must be taken into account during the work.
- Agreed start and delivery dates and the hours and/or costs involved.
- Limiting conditions and assumptions.
- Standards and procedures to be met.
- Reporting requirements, how often and when.
- Change and escalation procedure.
- Configuration management requirements.
- Agreements concerning the delivery and hand-over of products.

The Work Package contains all the Product Descriptions relating to the deliverables. Included in the Products Descriptions are the quality requirements, how the product is to be checked and by whom.

The Team Manager must set up a team plan and carry out a risk analysis in order to take on a Work Package in a responsible manner. Here the Team Manager makes use of the process Planning (PL). Ideally, the Team Manager will have been involved in creating a Stage Plan and has set up a team plan (outline) so that when Accepting a Work Package the Team Manager needs only to update the team plan. The Team manager discusses the team plan and the risks with the Project Manager.

The input for the subprocess is the receipt of a Work Package. During the process, the team plan and the Risk Log are updated. The output of the subprocess is the agreed Work Package.

Executing a Work Package (MP2)

This subprocess describes the delegation and management of the work needed for execution of the Work Package.

The Team Manager's activities comprise:
- Managing the activities within the constraints of the budget, agreed timescale and quality.
- Monitoring the risks throughout the execution process.
- Escalating Project Issues to the Project Manager.
- Carrying through agreed changes, if necessary.
- Testing the deliverables and update the Quality Log.
- Providing Checkpoint Reports.

This subprocess makes use of the agreed Work Package. During this subprocess the Team Manager updates the team plan based upon work progress. Interim adaptations to the team plan may be necessary in order to be able to deliver the work on time, within budget and in agreement with the agreed quality. The Team Manager puts the results of the tests carried out in the Quality Log. The Team Manager reports periodically to the Project Manager using the Check-point report. The output of the subprocess is the completed Work Package.

Delivering a Work Package (MP3)

This process describes the Work Package to be delivered to the Project Manager.

The Team Manager's activities comprise:
- Delivering of the completed products.
- Notifying the Project Manager of delivery of the completed products.
- Handing-over of the completed products and ensuring that all relevant documents, records and files are updated.
- Ensuring that the completed Work Package is signed by the Project Manager.

The Team Manager delivers the completed products to the Project Manager whilst ensuring that the products are accepted by the users. Acceptance and testing/approval are different matters. Acceptance of the completed products is the result of testing and approval of the products in the subprocess MP2. By involving the users in MP2 in product testing the Team Manager is able to ensure that user acceptance of the products is a smooth process.

When the Work Package is executed by third parties, then signing off the completed Work Package by the Project Manager is often a precondition to sending an invoice and getting an invoice paid.

Input for the subprocess is the completed Work Package. Output of the subprocess is the delivery of a Work Package.

3.6.4 Input and output

Table 5 gives the input and output of all subprocesses in the process Managing Product Delivery.

Managing Product Delivery (MP)

Input	Subprocess	Output
• Work Package • Team Plan • Risk Log	MP1 Accepting a Work Package	• Approved Work Package • Team Plan (update) • Risk Log (update)
• Approved Work Package • Team Plan • Quality Log	MP2 Executing a Work Package	• Checkpoint Report • Completed Work Package • Team Plan (update) • Quality Log (update)
• Completed Work Package	MP3 Delivering a Work Package	• Approved Work Package

Table 5 Input and output MP

3.6.5 Responsibilities

The Team Manager is responsible for this process. The Team Manager is responsible for accepting a Work Package, for its execution, having the work package checked and for the hand-over of the completed Work Package to the Project Manager. The Team Manager is also responsible for updating the various documents and for liaising with the Configuration Librarian about the status of the Configuration Item Records.

3.7 Managing Stage Boundaries (SB)

3.7.1 Context

Before starting a new management stage, a Stage Plan must be created for the next stage. The Project Plan, Risk Log and Business Case for the project must be updated and approval given for the last stage.

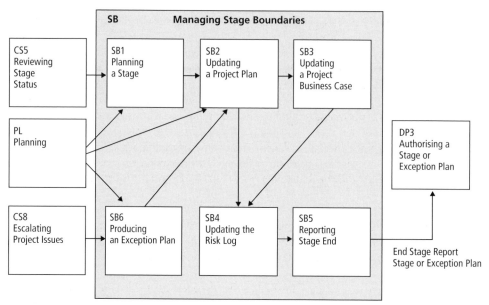

Figure 3.9 Managing Stage Boundaries (Source: OGC)

The process Managing Stage Boundaries is triggered by the subprocess Reviewing Stage Status (CS5) or by the subprocess Escalating Project Issues (CS8). For different subprocesses in the process Managing Stage Boundaries use is made of the process Planning (PL). The process Managing Stage Boundaries provides the input for the End Stage Assessment of the Project Board in the subprocess Authorising a Stage or Exception Plan (DP3) (see figure 3.9).

3.7.2 Fundamental principles

This process describes the activities that must be carried out by the Project Manager in preparation for the Project Board's no go/go decisions in DP3. During the End Stage Assessment the Project Board decides whether it is expedient to stop the project or to allow it to continue, and if so, whether it should continue unchanged.

3.7.3 Process description

The objectives of the process Managing Stage Boundaries are to:
- Assure the Project Board that all products in the previous stage have been completed as agreed.
- Provide the Project Board with information that confirms the project's viability.
- Provide the Project Board with the Stage Plan for the next stage, including the agreed tolerances and required commitment of people and resources for the next stage.
- Identify the lessons learned from the previous stage that can assist the progress of a following project and provide the basis for the Lessons Learned Report to be compiled at the end of the project.

Based on the information given about the viability of the project the Project Board is able to make a decision concerning the no go/go of the project. Based on the Stage Plan for the next stage, the Project Board can authorise the next stage to start and commit the required people and resources for the next stage. Based on the End Stage Report the Project Board can discharge the Project Manager and his project team for the work performed in the previous stage.

Planning a Stage (SB1)

The Stage Plan for the next stage must have enough detail to act as a basis for the Project Manager's day-to-day control of the stage. The Stage Plan must contain all the specialist products needed to execute the next stage. Product Descriptions must be provided for these products and/or updated. The Stage Plan must also contain all the control documents, such as the information for delivery of the Check-point Reports and the Highlight Reports. The Stage Plan must also contain all the checks and any other activities within the framework of quality control descriptions and planning, including the required commitment of people and resources.

The Project Manager must check that all activities within the framework of quality control meet with those of Project Assurance. For all the deliverables in this stage, Project Assurance must be consulted on who will represent the various parties in the Project Board at the various quality reviews.

This subprocess makes use of the PID, the updated Stage Plan of the current stage, the Issue Log and Risk Log. The output of this subprocess is the draft Stage Plan for the next stage. The subprocess SB1 may lead to the Issue Log and Risk Log being updated.

It is best to implement any changes in the Project Management Team during management of stage boundaries. If necessary, the management structure and job descriptions must be updated.

Updating a Project Plan (SB2)

The Project Board uses the Project Plan throughout the lifecycle of the project in order to assess progress. It is therefore important for the Project Plan to be updated at each stage boundary. This provides the Project Board members with an overview of the latest position and gives a forecast of the portion of the project still to be executed. The updated Project Plan acts as a basis for updating the project Business Case (SB3). An explanation about any changes to the Project Plan is included in the End Stage Report.

This subprocess makes use of the updated Stage Plan for the current stage, the Stage Plan for the next stage or the Exception Plan, current Project Plan, Project Approach, Project Quality Plan, Issue Log and the Risk Log. The output of this subprocess is the updated Project Plan. The subprocess SB2 can also lead to an update of the Issue Log and the Risk Log.

Updating a Project Business Case (SB3)

Throughout the project it is necessary to keep a focus on the Business Case. Each time during managing stage boundaries the validity of the Business Case must again be checked.

Important aspects for the Business Case are updating costs, the planning and the important risks of the project. It is also important to include any external factors. When updating the Business Case, a check must also be made of what is included in the Issue Log and Risk Log.

A delay in the project delivery could have a serious impact on the validity of the Business Case.

Delays in delivery can lead to:
- Increased development costs.
- Shorter production learning curve.
- Loss of market share.
- Shorter return period (in relation to the life of the product).
- Weakening of competitive position.

If the Business Case has become less valid, the chairman of the Project Board must advise this to the corporate or programme management. It is corporate or programme management that will finally determine whether the project is still sufficiently viable for the company's internal standards.

The Project Manager is not responsible for the Business Case, but does have delegated responsibility for monitoring the Business Case. Once again, it is not just the costs, time and risks but the benefits forecast that must be checked carefully. The Project Manager may be assisted by Project Support and by those from Project Assurance responsible for the business. Monitoring the benefits is primarily the customer's responsibility.

The Project Plan and the Stage Plan for the next stage, or the Exception Plan, form the input for the subprocess Updating a Project Business Case. This subprocess can lead to the Issue Log and Risk Log being updated or even changes to the Stage or Exception Plan and Project Plan.

Updating the Risk Log (SB4)
Risks change during the life of the project. That is why risks must be regularly reviewed. According to PRINCE2, risk analysis forms a standard part of the process Planning (PL) and is part of the subprocess Updating a Project Business Case (SB3). Whilst preparing for the no go/go decision-making within the management of stage boundaries it is, however, extremely important that the risks are all assessed individually and the Risk Log updated accordingly. Whilst risk analysis is aimed at a certain section during the PL process and subprocess SB3, the objective of risk analysis in the subprocess SB4 is to analyse the risks to the project as a whole. These risks include both internal and external project risks.

This subprocess makes use of the Risk Log, Business Case, Project Plan, Stage Plan or the Exception Plan. This subprocess can also lead to the Issue Log being updated and to even more changes being made to the Stage or Exception Plan and Project Plan.

Reporting Stage End (SB5)
For each stage, responsibility must reside with those who have made the commitment of people and resources possible and those who have approved execution of the stage. This responsibility is presented in the End Stage Report. This report must be compiled as close as possible to the stage end.

The End Stage Report compares the end results of the stage in terms of time, costs and products produced within the original Stage Plan and agreed tolerances. Furthermore, this report explains the validity of the project in relation to the Project Plan, Business Case and the risks identified. This report also gives an overview of the activities that have been carried out within the framework of quality control and the results of this. Additionally, an overview is given of all the Project Issues registered during the last stage.

A configuration audit is performed to identify whether the configuration items agree with the information given in the configuration management database. Learning points are put into the Lessons Learned Log for the next stages and form a basis for the Lessons Learned Report to be compiled at a later date.

The Project Manager sends the End Stage Report with the Business Case, Project Plan and Stage or Exception Plan to the Project Board for assessment and approval, together with the request for authorisation to start with the next stage. The Project Manager also informs third parties as indicated in the Communication Plan.

This subprocess makes use of the current Stage Plan, updated Business Case, updated Project Plan, various log books, Communication Plan and the next Stage or Exception Plan. In this subprocess, the configuration management database and the Lessons Learned Log are updated. The output of this subprocess is the End Stage Report and the official request from the Project Manager to start with the next stage.

Producing an Exception Plan (SB6)

As soon as there is a threat that one or more tolerances of a stage and/or project will be exceeded, the Project Manager must escalate this to the Project Board by means of an Exception Report. Based on this Exception Report, the Project Board will decide how to proceed with the project or whether to stop the project. If there is still a valid Business Case, the Project Board in consultation with corporate or programme management can decide whether or not to continue the project in a different form. The Project Board gives the Project Manager the assignment to produce the chosen scenario in an Exception Plan and to prepare for the formal no go/go decision of the Project Board. The Project Manager then triggers an early start of the process Managing Stage Boundaries.

In this accelerated version of Managing Stage Boundaries, the first step is to produce an Exception Plan for the remaining part of the current stage. This replaces the Stage Plan for the next stage (SB1). The other subprocesses of this accelerated version are identical to the original process Managing Stage Boundaries. The Exception Plan includes the same setup and details as the original plan it replaces, with the addition of the Exception Report which led to the production of the Exception Plan.

It is important to carefully check the actual status of the Configuration Items when producing an Exception Plan. Work outstanding in the current stage must be included in the Exception Plan. An Exception Plan can be produced for a Stage Plan and for a Project Plan.

This subprocess makes use of the current Stage Plan, approved Exception Report, Issue Log and Risk Log. The output of this subprocess is the Draft Exception Plan.

3.7.4 Input and output

Table 6 gives the input and output of all the subprocesses of the process Managing Stage Boundaries.

Input	Subprocess	Output
• Stage end notification • Current Stage Plan • Project Initiation Document • Issue Log • Risk Log • Project management team structure	SB1 Planning a Stage	• Next Stage Plan • Project Management Team structure (update)
• Project Plan • Project Quality Plan • Project Approach • Next Stage Plan/Exception Plan • Issue Log • Current Stage Plan	SB2 Updating a Project Plan	• Project Plan (update) • Project Quality Plan (update) • Project Approach (update) • Next Stage Plan/Exception Plan • Issue Log (update)
• Business Case • Next Stage Plan/Exception Plan • Risk Log • Project Plan • Issue Log	SB3 Updating a Project Business Case	• Business Case (update) • Next Stage Plan/Exception Plan • Risk Log (update
• Risk Log • Project Plan • Next Stage Plan/Exception Plan • Issue Log • Business Case	SB4 Updating the Risk Log	• Risk Log (update) • Project Plan (update) • Next Stage Plan/Exception Plan • Issue Log (update)
• Current Stage Plan • Next Stage Plan/Exception Plan • Business Case • Issue and Risk Log • Quality Log • Communication Plan	SB5 Reporting Stage End	• Request for authorisation to proceed • End Stage Report • Next Stage Plan/Exception Plan • Lessons Learned Log (update) • Configuration Item Records • Status information to third parties
• Current Stage Plan • Issue Log • Risk Log • Approved Exception Plan	SB6 Producing an Exception Plan	• Exception Plan • Approved Exception Report

Table 6 Input and output SB

3.7.5 Responsibilities

The Project Manager is responsible for this process. The Project Manager can get support from the Team Managers, Project Support and the Configuration Librarian. The Team Managers, in particular, must provide the basic information for the next Stage Plan. The Configuration Librarian performs the configuration audit in order to ensure that the configuration items agree with the information in the configuration management database.

Those responsible for Project Assurance must ensure that the various documents for this process include the right information and meet the needs and expectations of the various project stakeholders. The customer is primarily responsible for checking what the benefits forecast will be and if any changes are expected. Those responsible for the various risks must indicate whether any changes are expected.

3.8 Closing a Project (CP)

3.8.1 Context

In general, the process of Closing a Project is triggered by the subprocess Reviewing Stage Status (CS5). If a project no longer has a good Business Case and is closed prematurely, the process Closing a Project is triggered by a direct decision from the Project Board. This can take place from the subprocess Authorising a Stage or Exception Plan (DP3) or from the subprocess Giving Ad Hoc Direction (DP4). The various subprocesses of the process Closing a Project can run in parallel.

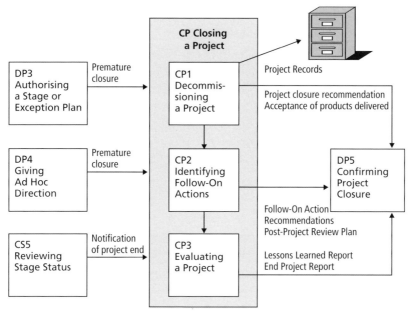

Figure 3.10 Closing a Project (Based on: OGC source)

Closing a Project is often planned as a separate stage in a project. Closing a Project, however, as defined by PRINCE2, does not form a separate management stage of the project. The process Closing a Project is 'only' a process and can be carried out at the end of the last management stage. This process can take place in parallel with the process Controlling a Stage and the process Managing a Product Delivery in the last management stage.

Often the decision to close a project is formally put before the Project Board. The Project Manager cannot trigger the process Closing a Project from CS5 without formal approval from the Project Board. This formal decision, however, does not make the process Closing a Project a separate management stage. The process Closing a Project provides the input for the decision by the Project Board to end the project in the subprocess Confirming Project Closure (DP5) (see figure 3.10).

3.8.2 Fundamental principles

A project needs a definite start and end. Without a good project closure, a large proportion of the support base built up and acceptance of the project outcome will be lost. This process describes the activities that must be carried out by the Project Manager so that the Project Board can bring the project to a proper conclusion.

3.8.3 Process description

In the process Closing a Project, the Project Manager must ensure that:

- What was agreed has actually been carried out in accordance with the agreements.
- The project outcome meets the Acceptance Criteria and that the project outcome and all the relevant documentation have been delivered and handed-over to corporate or programme management.
- A control and support organisation is in place for the project outcome.
- That any follow-on actions and recommendations have been identified.
- Learning points of the project have been recorded.
- The End Project Report has been prepared including project accountability.
- The post-project review has been planned.
- The project organisation has been disbanded.
- The project files have been archived in an orderly manner.

If the project outcome acts as input for a subsequent project, then it is not necessary to have a control and support organisation in place for the project outcome. With premature closure of the project, parts of the process Closing a Project will be cancelled.

Decommissioning a Project (CP1)

The Project Manager must ensure that the project outcome meets the Acceptance Criteria and that all project outcomes have been handed over to and accepted by both the end users and those responsible for operation and maintenance of the project outcome. The Project Manager must investigate in advance whether the necessary operation and support organisation for the project outcome is in place. Furthermore, the Project Manager must ensure that the project files are complete and stored. The Project Manager must also check whether all Project Issues have been dealt with. Any open Project Issues must be included in the Follow-on Action Recommendations (see CP3).

End users and those responsible for operation and maintenance often belong to different parties in an organisation. The Project Manager must ensure that both parties' specifications are met and that the project outcome is accepted by both parties. It is recommended that both parties sign the delivery protocol separately. Actual hand-over of the project outcome is usually to the organisation responsible for the operation and maintenance.

The project team and project organisation must be disbanded. The actual instruction for this cannot be given by the Project Manager; it needs to come from a Project Board instruction, which is prepared by the Project Manager. In view of contractual agreements made with suppliers, it is often necessary for such an instruction to be given at an early stage. This is not without risk. It is possible that the suppliers will not be ready in time and that the instruction arrives too early. It is therefore recommended that the time and content of the instruction be tailored suitably to the various parties.

It is possible that the Project Manager may need to inform other stakeholders that the project is about to close, as laid down in the Communication Plan. The Project Manager must consult with the Project Board prior to this communication. The Project Board has final responsibility within the project for all external communications.

In addition to the formal side of disbanding the project, the Project Manager must also have a feel for the informal side. Many Project Managers pay a lot of attention to building a team, but forget to pay attention to correct decommissioning of the project organisation. Decommissioning a project team takes place by organising a drink or dinner for example, but could also be a joint project evaluation. Each project is different. For external parties it is often the case that the team members no longer see each other (at least for a while) after a project closure, whilst a relationship has formed between the team members. A project end always means a change of work which leads to insecurity. Ensuring proper closure for team members means that they in turn will ensure that the project closes correctly.

Identifying Follow-on Actions (CP2)

Hardly any project ends without any outstanding unfinished business and/or any Follow-on Action Recommendations on how to continue when the project outcome is delivered, which need to be handed over to the organisation. Frequently lots of small Request for Changes are not approved by the Project Board at the project end but shifted to the operational stage. Important Project Issues can sometimes lead to a new project being started after project hand-over. Many open Project Issues relate to the operational stage or to projects following on from the current project.

These Project Issues must not be dismissed. If they are, this could lead to negative feelings from those triggering Project Issues. This must be avoided. That is why it is necessary to document Follow-on Action Recommendations.

Besides the document Follow-on Action Recommendations, it is important to assess the final benefits of the project against the costs. The project is driven by the Business Case, therefore it must also be determined if the Business Case has been realised. However, this is not possible immediately the project ends. The actual organisation must first use the project outcome and learn to work with it before the forecast benefits can be realised. This assessment of the added value no longer belongs to the project. The plan for such a measurement must be set up and agreed within the framework of the project. The Project Manager puts this plan into the Post-Project Review Plan for agreement from the Project Board.

The various parties often do not look forward to a review. In practice, however, it has become apparent that a review offers advantages both to the customer and the supplier. Should the forecast benefits not be realised, then actions can be taken. A review also provides important learning points for new projects. If it becomes apparent that the product has not brought the benefits expected, a review can help find the cause. Often it is not the product itself, but its use. A review can therefore prevent the blame being laid with the supplier. A post-project review may start a following project. Stating that a post-project review will be held in the PID gives a good impression and can even provide the reason for working together with a certain supplier.

This subprocess makes use of the Issue Log, Risk Log and Business Case. The output of this subprocess is the document Follow-on Action Recommendations and the draft Post-Project Review Plan.

Project Evaluation Review (CP3)

The performance of a project must always be evaluated. Is the outcome what was agreed and if otherwise, what was originally agreed, how did that happen? How was the project controlled and what should or should not be done next time? Both questions are dealt with in an evaluation at the end of a project. Both questions approach matters from a different angle.

The answer to the question "Are the project results what was intended and if not, why not?" indicates the effectiveness of the project. This effectiveness is defined in an End Project Report. The End Project Report is compiled by the Project Manager for the Project Board, but is also used by the Project Board in reporting its effectiveness to corporate or programme management. In the End Project Report, the Project Plan is updated with the state of affairs at the project end and a comparison is made between what was originally agreed and the interim changes agreed. Furthermore, an overview is included in the End Project Report of the changes recorded including an evaluation of the total impact of approved changes to the project. Finally, an overview is included in the report of the quality assessments carried out.

People quickly forget everything that happened, why matters proceeded as they did and where they themselves were involved. If the Project Manager does not record this, then someone else will, or worse still, it remains unrecorded. The effect of this may turn out worse than if the report is compiled by the Project Manager himself. Therefore, it is recommended that the Project Manager compile this report so that the individual Project Board members are able to use this report when reporting to their corporate or programme management. The End Project Report is an important instrument for maintaining the support-base built up during the project as well as for determining the effectiveness of the project for the Project Manager and Project Board.

The answer to the question "How was the project controlled and what should or should not be done next time?" provides corporate or programme management with important learning points for the setup and execution of future projects. Learning points are recorded in a Lessons Learned Report. To capture learning points, use is made of the learning points recorded in the Lessons Learned Log. In addition, it is recommended that a separate evaluation of learning points for the complete project takes place at the end of the project. This defines the learning points from the previous management stage as well as evaluating all learning points recorded to date in the Lessons Learned Log. Sometimes new learning points are brought to the table which have not yet been recorded, or earlier learning points in the broader project context still need to be changed. An evaluation of learning points at the end of the project is an excellent means of closing the project for the project team.

In the Lessons Learned Report an evaluation is included of what went well and what could have gone better with regard to management and quality control processes and methods and techniques. In addition, an evaluation is included of specialist work. It is important that special project circumstances are also included in the Lessons Learned Report in order to ensure that account is taken of this during evaluation. Furthermore, the recommendations for following projects must be clearly specified. Finally, statistics giving the time, commitment and costs, and an evaluation of the quality reviews carried out are included in the report. The learning points are important for the various organisations within the corporate organisation. It may therefore be necessary to make several copies of the Lessons Learned Report.

This subprocess makes use of the PID, various logs, Project Quality Plan and the Configuration management database. The output of this process is the End Project Report and the Lessons Learned Report.

3.8.4 Input and output

Table 7 gives the input and output of all subprocesses of the process Closing a Project.

Closing a Project (CP)

Input	Subprocess	Output
• Notification of project end • Decision for premature closure • Project Initiation Document • Configuration Item Records • Communication Plan	CP1 Decommissioning a Project	• Acceptance by end user of the deliverables • Acceptance by operations and maintenance of the deliverables • Project closure recommendation • Project Files
• Business Case • Issue Log • Risk Log	CP2 Identifying Follow-on Actions	• Post-Project Review Plan • Follow-on Action Recommendations
• Project Initiation Document • Issue Log • Risk Log • Project Quality Plan • Configuration Item Records • Lessons Learned Log	CP3 Evaluating a Project	• End Project Report • Lessons Learned Report

Table 7 Input and output CP

3.8.5 Responsibilities

The Project Manager is responsible for this process. The Project Manager can be supported here by Project Support and the Configuration Librarian. The Configuration Librarian does a configuration audit in order to ensure that the configuration items agree with the information in the configuration management database. For the subprocess Evaluating a Project the Project Manager must consult with the Team Managers.

The Project Manager consults on an informal basis with the various Project Board members in order to ensure that no unexpected problems occur with the closure of the project.

Those responsible for Project Assurance must ensure that the various documents from this process are correct and meet the needs and expectations of the various stakeholders in the project and that the project can actually be closed.

3.9 Planning (PL)

3.9.1 Context

The Planning process is driven by the following subprocesses:

- SU6   Planning an Initiation Stage   Stage Plan
- IP2   Planning a Project   Project Plan
- MP1   Accepting a Work Package   team plan
- SB1   Planning a Stage   Stage Plan
- SB2   Updating a Project Plan   Project Plan
- SB6   Producing an Exception Plan   Exception Plan

Furthermore, the Planning process is used in the processes, which are an adaptation of the various plans that the subprocess brings. Within the subprocess Updating a Project Business Case (SB3) the Project Plan is updated, also making use of the Planning process.

Planning is an iterative process. In practice, the various subprocesses take place not just once, but several times, often with increased attention to detail. The various subprocesses are directly related and take place together (see figure 3.11).

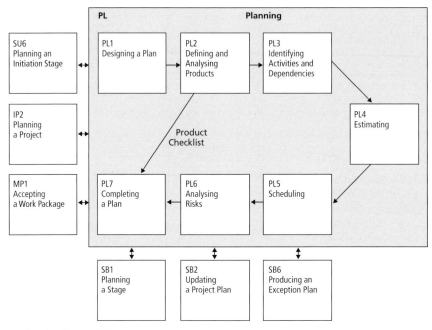

Figure 3.11 Planning (Source: OGC)

3.9.2 Fundamental principles

Planning is an essential part of the control process. It is needed in both small and large projects. Plans must be constructed at every level of the project, so including at project level and per stage as well as per Work Package.

A plan is not just a time schedule. A plan must give:
• What the outcome of the plan is to be.
• How this outcome is to be achieved.
• Who, when and how it must be carried out.
• The required commitment of people and resources.
• The costs involved.

Because plans must be constructed on several levels within a project in the various stages and in the various subprocesses, Planning is defined as a separate process in the form of a separate subroutine that takes place within more processes. Due to the importance of this process in project management this process is defined as the main process within PRINCE2.

Where required, Plans can be combined. It will also not always be necessary to make separate Stage Plans and Team Plans for small projects.

3.9.3 Process description

The Planning process is product-based. It is not possible to have a clear understanding of the work to be carried out or the time-scale and costs involved without first determining which products must be produced and delivered, the content of these products, what comes next and the interrelationship of the products.

Only once this has been determined and the description of the deliverables as well as what comes next has been determined, can the activities necessary to develop the products and services be determined. Based on this a good assessment can be made of the costs and the required commitment of people and resources. Based on this, a comparison can be made between which people and resources are available and what is required so that the timing can be planned and a plan can be made. A separate risk analysis of the plan is required to determine and estimate the risks involved in the plan. Based on this analysis, the plan is further optimised. It may be necessary to run through the planning processes again. Only once the plan and the remaining risks are brought into balance can the plan be finalised and compiled as a definite document (see figure 3.12).

Designing a Plan (PL1)

Before Planning can be started the layout and the amount of detail must first be determined. This is determined by the Project Board. Also to be agreed is the planning approach to be used, which software tool must be used and which notation system is to be used. Whether the project is to be carried out within a programme or within a project organisation determines many of these aspects before the start of the project and the subprocess for the initiation stage can then be run through faster.

It is important that the setup, layout and detail of the various plans in the project are determined together. Are several planning levels needed or will one or two planning levels suffice? What do the various parties at the various levels within the Project Management Team want and need to know and what level of detail is needed per planning level? Usually this adjustment takes place only once within a project and at the start of planning the Project Plan.

The setup, layout and detail are extremely important both to the time planning and the estimate and budget of the plan. Often standard layouts for estimates are used for projects within one organisation. These layouts make it possible to determine the detailed costs at the end of the project, which may be of use in following projects.

This subprocess also determines how to deal with change budgets and contingency budgets or risk budgets. Are these budgets allocated separately and if so, at which planning level? In some organisations, separate risk budgets are not determined but the permitted tolerances are raised, with others, risk budgets are allocated in the team plans or allocated in the Stage Plans under the Project Manager's control or a combination of both is applied.

The Project Board is ultimately responsible for the design of the plans within the project. In practice, however, the Project Manager usually determines the design of the various plans at the same time and advises the Project Board. As indicated, it is often the case that the various plan designs within a project have already been laid down by the corporate or programme organisation.

This subprocess makes use of the Project Approach, Project Quality Plan, Project Brief or the PID and company planning standards. The output of the subprocess is a plan design.

Defining and Analysing Products (PL2)

The quality of a plan improves greatly if the deliverables are first identified and described, and the sequence in which the products are to be produced is defined.

This subprocess is divided into the following steps:
- Identify the products to be realised and delivered.
- Describe each of the separate products.
- Determine the order in which the products are to be produced.

The products to be produced are identified using a product breakdown. The specialist products and the management products must be included in the product breakdown. For large and complex projects, product breakdowns must be compiled for the separate parts. It is recommended that a separate Product List be compiled with all the products to be developed in order to maintain an overview of all the products that must be produced.

The Product Descriptions are defined for each product. A Product Description contains:
- The objective, why the product is needed.
- The materials and documents required to produce the product.
- Those responsible for producing the product.
- The product composition.
- The quality criteria and manner in which the product must be tested in order to check that it meets the criteria and who performs it.

The sequence in which the products must be developed is defined in a Product Flow Diagram.

Within this subprocess, use is made of the technique Product-based planning. This technique is described further in chapter 5 of this book.

This subprocess makes use of the plan design and the Project Quality Plan. The output of this subprocess is a Product Breakdown Structure, Product Descriptions of the individual products, Product Checklist (optional) and the Product Flow Diagram.

Identifying Activities and Dependencies (PL3)

Product-based planning alone may supply insufficient information for further planning of the project and monitoring of the progress. The activities required must be identified in order to develop the individual products AND assess the interrelationships between these activities and possible external dependencies.

With the identification of the required activities a look must be taken at the risks included in the Risk Log. Are there any risks that could be involved in these products, have measures been identified that must be included in the activities?

Project Plans and Stage Plans are usually represented at product level. In the team plans for the various Work Packages the deliverables are usually further subdivided into the required activities. Within planning, every product to be delivered is considered a milestone, including the activities required to produce the product. These activities can be represented in the various detail plans.

Often new products are identified in the analysis of the required activities in order to develop new products that must be produced and for which the progress and quality must be monitored during execution. If that is the case the subprocess PL3 reaches back to the subprocess PL2.

The activities identified are easier to present in a list with the dependencies of other activities and external dependencies behind them. External dependencies may be products required from another Work Package or even from another project, which can have a bearing on decisions that need to be taken by the Project Board or by corporate or programme management.

This subprocess makes use of the Product Flow Diagram, Product Descriptions and Risk Log. The output of this subprocess is an activity list with the internal and external dependencies.

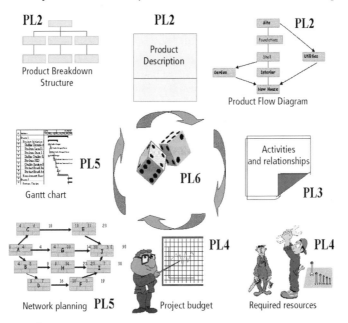

Figure 3.12 Subprocess results

Estimating (PL4)

Making an estimate cannot be accurate by definition. However, it is always better to make an estimate than not at all. Making estimates is the responsibility of the Project Manager and/or Team Manager and comprises:
- Estimating the amount of the various products to be produced.
- Identifying the required commitment of people and resources.
- Making an estimate of the expected costs.
- Estimating the duration times of the individual activities.

First of all a project top-down breakdown of the products to be produced is divided into the activities required followed by a division of the required commitment of people and resources and other costs. The breakdown of larger projects is usually first divided per stage or per location. Standardised classifications and checklists are usually used in order to ensure that specific activities and costs are not forgotten, such as external costs for the delivery of services from third parties, costs for use of the facilities, general services and travel and accommodation expenses.

Subsequently, the numbers of products to be produced is determined together with the productivity standard per cost type for the various activities, the required resource per cost type per activity and, if necessary, the costs per unit resource per cost type, the costs per cost type per activity and finally, the total costs per product, per stage and for the complete plan. In some organisations, separate estimates are made for the hours to be employed and the external costs. In general, the hours to be employed are also calculated into costs and a complete estimate is made of the hours to be employed together with the costs for each project. For estimating the commitment of people and resources, it is recommended that use be made of productivity standards developed from previous projects. It must not be forgotten to check of the commitment of people and resources for assessing the products.

Besides estimating the costs, an estimate is also made of the duration time and the individual activities in this subprocess. This estimate assumes availability of the required resource and expected/desired commitment of people and resources per activity.

> *Duration time = required resource / commitment*

The subprocesses PL2 and PL3 provide the input for this subprocess. The output of this subprocess are estimates for the amount of products to be produced, the required commitment of people and resources, expected duration time, the estimate for the individual activities and an estimate of the costs of the complete plan.

Scheduling (PL5)
In addition to estimating the commitment of people and resources, the total duration time of a plan must be determined as well as a specification of when each activity is to be carried out. Both can be determined by drawing up a time schedule.

A time schedule is made based on the required/expected commitment of people and resources per activity. It is strongly recommended that use be made here of a network plan in combination with a Gantt chart.

Resulting from this, the simultaneous commitment of people and resources for the complete project must subsequently be determined and set against the resource available. Should it become apparent from this comparison that less resource is available than required at any period in the project then additional resource must be acquired or the time schedule adapted. A check must first be made as to whether it is possible to shift those activities not lying at a critical point in the path, or to spread them out over a longer period or divide them into smaller units in order to lower the demand for resource at one point. Should any this not lead to the desired result, then the total duration time of the plan must be changed. If necessary, the cost estimate of the plan will also need to be changed accordingly.

Finally, periodical control activities must be added to the timing can be planned as well as the Check-point Reports, Highlight Reports and the management of stage boundaries.

Analysing Risks (PL6)
Producing a plan without simultaneously evaluating the risks that come with the activities to be carried out in the plan immediately puts execution of the plan into danger. Analysing such risks must take place throughout the Planning process. Each assumption has a risk: is this assumption correct, is the assumption on the safe side or not and to what extent in reality is it actually

dependent on other factors? During the whole PL process, the risks of each assumption and each decision must be anticipated.

Apart from this continuous attention to risks during the Planning process, the plan must be completely analysed again for all such risks at the end of this process. How certain is it that certain capacities will actually become available, are there too many critical activities in the complete plan, how much time has been built in order to change the products if, on checking the products, it is found that they do not meet the specifications, what are the consequences for illness with certain team members? Usually, such a risk analysis at the end of the PL process provides the reason for going through the process once again and working out alternative solutions. Only once sufficient balance has been found between the plan and the risks that go with it can the plan be considered complete. The Risk Log is updated based on the remaining risks.

The previous subprocesses in the PL process provide the input for this subprocess. The outcome of this subprocess is the Risk Log update.

Completing a Plan (PL7)

A plan mustn't simply consist of a number of diagrams, time schedules and estimates. The approach, starting points and assumptions that form the basis for the plan must be given for each plan. Without this information the plan has little value. Plans without an infrastructure can lead to differences of opinion with later changes to the plan. The management level receiving the reports is unable to assess the plan or any alternatives without such an infrastructure and the Project Manager or Team Manager is also unable to monitor the progress of the plan adequately.

Once again the plan must be checked for completeness and to ensure that all the components link together correctly. The margins of the individual activities and the tolerances for the complete plan must again be confirmed, tailored to and in agreement with the management receiving the reports. A final check must be carried out as to whether all the required quality checks have also been planned for (with regard to the required commitment of people and resources, the costs and time required for this). The Product Checklist must be completed by adding the planned start and end dates per product.

3.9.4 Input and output

Table 8 gives the input and output of all the subprocesses of the Planning process.

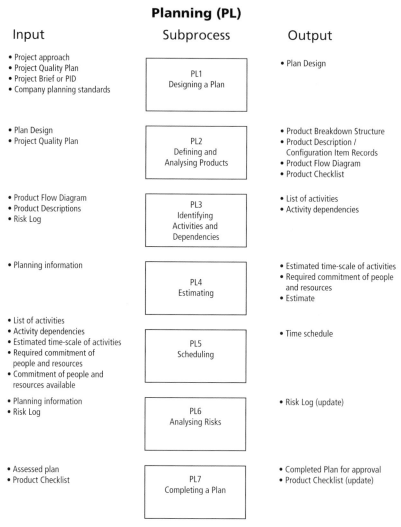

Planning (PL)

Input	Subprocess	Output
• Project approach • Project Quality Plan • Project Brief or PID • Company planning standards	PL1 Designing a Plan	• Plan Design
• Plan Design • Project Quality Plan	PL2 Defining and Analysing Products	• Product Breakdown Structure • Product Description / Configuration Item Records • Product Flow Diagram • Product Checklist
• Product Flow Diagram • Product Descriptions • Risk Log	PL3 Identifying Activities and Dependencies	• List of activities • Activity dependencies
• Planning information	PL4 Estimating	• Estimated time-scale of activities • Required commitment of people and resources • Estimate

• List of activities
• Activity dependencies
• Estimated time-scale of activities
• Required commitment of
  people and resources
• Commitment of people and
  resources available
	PL5
	Scheduling
		• Time schedule

• Planning information • Risk Log	PL6 Analysing Risks	• Risk Log (update)
• Assessed plan • Product Checklist	PL7 Completing a Plan	• Completed Plan for approval • Product Checklist (update)

Table 8 Input and output PL

3.9.5 Responsibilities

In the Planning process, the Project Manager is responsible for setting up the Project Plan and Stage Plans. The Team Managers are responsible for setting up the team plans in alignment with the Project Manager.

Those who are responsible for Project Assurance must take care that all the products to be produced and to be delivered are identified and that the plans are intrinsically correct. The Project Manager and Team Managers can be supported by Project Support.

Furthermore, it is recommended that the people who will ultimately carry out the work in the Planning be involved, such as the Team Managers and team members, and that those responsible for the commitment of these people such as the Senior Supplier, resource managers or department heads should also be involved.

The Configuration Librarian makes use of the results of this process in setting up and completing the configuration management database, insofar as is specified in the Configuration Management Plan. The Product Descriptions of the individual products are included in the configuration management database.

3.10 Small projects

3.10.1 Small projects and bureaucracy

Small projects are only too often stifled by too much paper and bureaucracy. Most organisational procedures and templates developed for the organisation and management of projects are based on large and complex projects. Many organisations are NEN-ISO certified. This certification requires evidence of management and specialist activities, which demands a lot of paperwork and the relevant signatures.

The PRINCE2 methodology can strengthen this because the method is extremely comprehensive and is underpinned by a large number of templates that can be used for organising and managing projects. In addition, all the available PRINCE2 templates are outlined or used in order to guarantee the feeling of maximum control of the project. An overkill of documents is more likely to distract attention from what is really going on and can lead to an aversion of all documents, even if a document is actually important. An overkill of documents also involves a lot of time and attention to produce and study them. This time and attention is better spent on other matters.

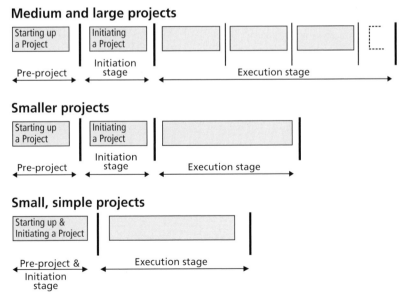

Figure 3.13 Stages of projects

All PRINCE2 processes must be considered for each project. The question is, however, whether all the processes in a given project are so important that specific procedures and templates for the execution of these processes are necessary. It is important to use only the procedures and templates in a project that are absolutely necessary for the given circumstances and that provide added value for the organisation and management of that project. For small and internal projects, certain processes can often be executed quickly and informally.

3.10.2 Large versus small projects

Medium and large projects have several execution stages besides the initiation stage. For short non-complex projects with limited risks, the project often has only two management stages: the initiation stage and the execution stage. For small and simple projects, the processes Starting Up a Project and Initiating a Project can often be combined. For small internal projects the management of the project can sometimes be dealt with informally. It is important to execute the processes, but to keep reporting to a minimum.

With many simple small informal projects the processes Starting Up a Project and Initiating a Project can sometimes be dealt with informally and at the same time in one meeting. It is recommended that any decisions made be recorded in the minutes of the meeting. This could be the case, for example, for small internal moves within a department or the like.

Whilst managing a project many decisions and reports are dealt with by oral arrangement. The Project Manager notes which decisions and reports are to be recorded in writing in order to avoid possible conflicts at a later stage.

For small projects the process Controlling a Stage can be summarised as follows:
- Assign work that needs to be carried out.
- Monitor the progress.
- Ensure that the quality agreed is achieved.
- Ensure that changes are made only after they have been approved.
- Monitor the risks.
- Report on the progress of the work.
- Keep an eye on any changes that might occur to plans.

These activities must take place even in the smallest of projects. However, the question remains whether the reporting of these activities must always be the same as in large reports. Simple reports may be sufficient or even oral reports for small and informal projects. The Project Management Team must, however, realise that oral reporting has its risks. Discussions may take place later concerning what was agreed. And, what happens when the Project Manager is temporarily out of circulation or leaves?

For small projects the PRINCE2 templates can be used, however, it may be decided not to use certain parts of them with the agreement of the Project Board

For small projects or projects with only one team reporting directly to the Project Manager, the regulation between the Project Manager and Team Manager may also be less formal. The work of the Team Manager can then be summarised as follows:
- Agrees the work that needs to be done.
- Plans the work.
- Supervises the execution.

- Monitors progress.
- Reports on progress.
- Have the products assessed.
- Record the results.
- Keep up to date with changes.
- Ensures that the products are in agreement.
- Delivers the products to the Project Manager.

For small projects the process Closing a Project can be summarised as follows:
- Check whether everything has been delivered and accepted.
- Check that there are no loose ends.
- Define any outstanding points.
- Archive the project files for assessment at a later stage.
- Sign off people and resources.

3.10.3 Project Manager versus Team Manager

Small projects often consist of one project team. Only project team members work on the project and they report directly to the Project Manager. This means one of two situations:
- The project is divided into separate Work Packages, but each of these Work Packages is carried out by one person. Each person functions as team member and Team Manager at the same time. In that case the Project Manager and Team Manager are separate people.
- The Project Manager does not control the team member at Work Package level but at activity level. This is necessary if the team member is not yet senior enough to carry out the Work Package independently and the Project Manager has the professional expertise in the area of work to be performed. In this case the Project Manager and Team Manager are one and the same person.

It is possible that within small projects both situations occur. With the second option, however, there is the danger that the team member concerned feels insufficiently involved and is therefore not proactive: "after all the Project Manager tells me what I have to do. It's his project/problem and not my project/problem". This happens, particularly if the team member has (as far as he is concerned) sufficient expertise to function as Team Manager, but is not given the responsibility. This is detrimental to team forming and the commitment within the team and only strengthens the risk of the Project Manager increasingly interfering in matters. The Project Manager interferes 'out of habit' in the work. Often the Project Manager is not used to controlling on the basis of Work Packages and continues to stick to the old ways of operating. Coaching by third parties is often necessary in order to avoid such situations, or to get out of such a situation.

4. Components

Besides the PRINCE2 process model, the methodology also describes eight components that act as building bricks in the various processes.

These components are:
- Business Case
- Organisation
- Plans
- Controls
- Management of Risk
- Quality in a Project Environment
- Configuration Management
- Change Control

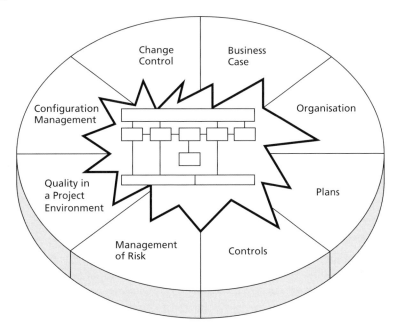

Figure 4.1 Circle of components (Based on: OGC source)

4.1 Business Case

One of the most important characteristics of PRINCE2 projects is the attention paid to the Business Case. The Business Case provides the practical justification for a project. It is essential for the success of a project to know the relationship between the cost of the project and the income, what the Executive intends achieving with the project outcome and how great the risks are. If the costs and the risks outweigh the expected benefits, there is no valid Business Case and there is therefore no reason to start the project.

If, during the execution of the project, it appears that there is no longer a valid Business Case, the project ought to be stopped. The project can only be continued in an alternative form if there is a positive Business Case for that alternative.

The Business Case must be prepared at the beginning of the project and must be regularly updated throughout the duration of the project. All the stakeholders in a project are expected to provide information that could prove important for the Business Case or for achieving the aims of the Business Case.

4.1.1 Which information should the Business Case contain?

The Business Case contains a description of the practical justification for carrying out the project, based on the costs and benefits of the project and the risks attached to it. When writing it, all changes that will occur as a result of taking the project outcome into use should be weighed up. Not just the immediate changes that will occur, but ALL the effects resulting from the project outcome.

The Business Case should at least explain and specify the following:
- **Reasons** - this is where details are given of the reasons for the project. These reasons must be described in the Project Mandate. If this is not done, the reasons will have to be worked out and described in the Project Brief during the SU process.
- **Options** - if a number of alternatives have been examined for achieving the Executive's reasons/aims described, these options should be described briefly, including the reasons for rejecting them. Always include the 'zero option': what happens if we do nothing? The preferred option must be indicated.
- **Benefits** - this contains a summary of the benefits/proceeds to be achieved by the deliverables. The various benefits must be formulated in a specific and measurable way. The benefits must always be defined with respect to the zero option. It is also important to give an estimate of when the benefit can be expected and how it can be measured. The disappearance/reduction of current income or an increase in current operating costs should also be included as benefits, but then as 'negative benefits'.
- **Risks** - a list of the most important risks that could have a considerable impact on the project. These might be risks relating to people, location, organisation, services and processes and not simply risks arising from infrastructure, data and applications.
  The details of the risks are given in the Risk Log and can be left out here.
- **Costs and timeline** - the Business Case must contain a list of the costs involved during execution of the project. It must also include the time when these costs will be incurred. This information can be gleaned from the Project Plan. It may be necessary to provide more details in the Business Case, especially if a phased budget is to be assigned to the project. This applies particularly to projects with a long duration time.
- **Application for investment** - this is the request for the project to be approved and thus for the execution of the project to be approved, based on consideration of the estimated costs, benefits and risks of the project. The main issue is the question of whether the expected benefits over the lifespan of the project justify the investment to be made in the project. That is why the benefits must be defined in a specific and measurable way.

There are many ways of drafting a Business Case. Often it depends on the standard used. It is also important to look at whether the project is highly dependent on one specific benefit. It may then be necessary to keep a particularly close eye on this benefit and to make specific agreements about it. For example, you might agree to pay extra attention to this aspect in the regular reports or to report on this benefit more frequently and specifically.

4.1.2 The customer's Business Case and that of the supplier

In a project, it is not only the customer who has a Business Case, but also the supplier. The supplier always needs to have a Business Case before taking part in the project. The supplier's Business Case is usually the return on the assignment itself, but may also be the expected increase in turnover in the long term. For example, if this project is a pilot project, or if the supplier can use the project to gain a stronger position in the market.

When the term Business Case is used in the context of a project, it usually refers to the customer's Business Case.

The customer's Business Case is often also called 'Total Cost of Ownership'. The supplier's Business Case is often referred to as the 'Integral Cost Price'. These terms are defined differently by different organisations and may therefore vary from the actual definition of a Business Case.

4.1.3 Developing the Business Case

The Business Case for a project is often written before a project starts. The first draft of a Business Case may be part of the annual process of producing the business plan for the organisation for the coming year(s). It may also be part of the Business Case for the programme of which the project is a part. Before the Programme Mandate is given, a feasibility study is often first carried out for the various options. A relevant Business Case is then drafted for each option, so that management can choose which project is to be carried out.

This means that there is often already a Business Case before the project starts. In such cases, the Business Case only has to be updated and worked out in detail in the project itself. However, it may be that, at the time of the project application (Project Mandate), there is no Business Case. In that case, the Business Case has to be written as part of the project.

The Executive is the owner of the Business Case and therefore responsible for its development. He examines the aim, costs, benefits and risks in the Business Case, and whether the Business Case is in line with the strategic aims of the line organisation or the programme. The Executive is also the person responsible for ensuring that the defined aims are actually achieved when the project outcome is delivered.

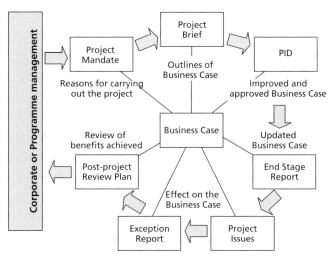

Figure 4.2 Business Case development path (Source: OGC)

The Project Manager may write the Business Case, but does not have to. It is, however, the Project Manager's job to see to it that there is a Business Case and to monitor the terms of reference of the Business Case for the Executive.

A large, complex project will require a group of specialists to write the Business Case. For a small project, one person should suffice. Sometimes it is better to arrange a meeting with all or some of the stakeholders to gather information for writing the Business Case. The Business Case continues to be worked out in detail and adjusted throughout the project.

Preparations for the project start are based on the Project Mandate. The customer should have given all the reasons why the project is needed in the Project Mandate. During project preparations, the Project Manager will record the outlines of the Business Case in the Project Brief (SU4) since these outlines form the basis on which the newly formed Project Board has to decide to authorise Project Initiation (DP1).

The Business Case will be worked out in detail or updated (IP3) in the initiation stage, based on the Project Plan and the risks indicated in the Risk Log. The results of the Business Case will be included in the PID (IP6). The Business Case must contain sufficient information for the Project Board to be able to make a well-considered decision as to whether there is sufficient basis for the project (DP2).

At the end of each management stage, the Project Manager will update the Business Case. The updated Business Case will be included in the End Stage Report (SB5) for the Project Board to make its decision (DP3).

The Project Manager will have to examine the consequences of all the Project Issues for the Business Case (CS4). In the event of an escalation, the Project Manager must examine the consequences of the escalation (and of the various options) for the Business Case and include them in his report to the Project Board (CS8). Based on this, the Project Board will eventually have to decide whether or not the project can continue and, if so, based on which scenario (DP4).

After completing the project, the Business Case will be used to verify whether the outcome of the project has resulted in the benefits forecast being achieved. Usually this cannot be established as soon as the project is delivered. The outcome has first to be in use for a while before it can be established whether the benefits forecast have actually been achieved. The Executive is responsible for the benefits actually being achieved. This must be shown by means of a post-project review. The Project Manager is responsible for designing a plan for the post-project review before the project is delivered.

4.2 Organisation

PRINCE2 assumes a customer-supplier relationship. The customer is a person or group that commissions the project and will profit from its outcome. The supplier produces the actual outcome of the project and makes people and resources available for this. The customer and the supplier may be part of the same organisation, but may also belong to different organisations.

PRINCE2 makes a distinction between the management of the project and those who are actually producing the specialist products. PRINCE2 focuses on the methodology and in particular on the management of the project. PRINCE2 furthermore assumes that the Project Manager is a member of the customer organisation, although this is not actually necessary. The distribution of roles would be the same if the Project Manager were a member of the supplier organisation. In the latter case, however, the customer will be less likely to assign responsibility for putting together the customer's Business Case to the Project Manager. The Project Manager remains nonetheless responsible for monitoring the Business Case on behalf of the Executive during the project.

A distinctive feature of a project is that it consists of a temporary management environment. Several disciplines from a number of functional units are often involved in working on the project. Often several people and parties in the customer organisation or the environment have a stake in the outcome of the project. To ensure the success of a project, it is necessary for it to be broadly established in the relevant line organisations. All this makes a connection between the project organisation and the relevant line organisations essential.

4.2.1 Project management structure

The management structure of a project contains four layers: corporate or programme management, the Project Board, the Project Manager and the Team Managers. Corporate or programme management is responsible for establishing corporate strategies, the Project Mandate, the mutual consultation between the various projects, the realisation of the benefits and the ultimate corporate aims. The corporate or programme management is also the entity that appoints the Executive and the Project Manager and that has to ratify the composition of the Project Board.

The Project Board is responsible for directing and managing the project. The corporate or programme management calls the Project Board to account on the success of the project and the Project Board carries final responsibility for the project within the mandate of the same corporate or programme management. The Project Manager is responsible for the day-to-day running of the project within the framework set by the Project Board. The Team Manager is responsible for directing the specialists and for producing the specialist products.

The Project Management Team for the project thus consists of the Project Board, the Project Manager and the Team Managers (plus any delegated Project Assurance and Project Support roles). The project organisation consists of the Project Management Team plus the project team members.

It is important that the roles in an organisation structure are described clearly and unambiguously and that they do not overlap. Each role in a project has its own tasks, authority and responsibilities, and interfaces with the other roles. Overlapping roles brings a lack of clarity and inefficiency. An unclear structure in a project can certainly lead to much confusion and time wasting. Figure 4.3 shows the project management structure, the Project Management Team and the project organisation.

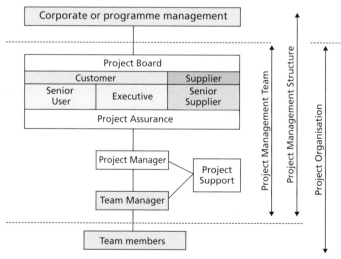

Figure 4.3 Project management structure (Based on: OGC source)

Some of the roles can be shared by several people, some cannot. Sometime one person or a group of people can take on several roles simultaneously, whilst other roles by definition must remain separate. More on this later in this chapter.

4.2.2 The three parties in a project

A standard feature of a project is that there are three sets of interests that have to be taken into account: the interests of the customer, the interests of the user and the interests of the supplier. All three must be represented in the management of the project to increase the chance of success.

> **The users**
> A new printer is to be installed in the Sales Department at Xanta. The printer will be placed in the corridor next to Rita's room. She has asthma. The department secretaries will use the printer. The account managers in the department need this new printer to be able to present their proposals more professionally. Xanta's customers had indicated that they did not like using the documentation they received from Xanta. The ink ran and made people's hands dirty, even after quite a long time. The new printer will be maintained by the company's own general and technical services department. All these parties have to be viewed as users. The users' representative who was involved in buying and placing the new printer had to take account of all these users' interests.

There are countless combinations of projects with all sorts of combinations of customers and suppliers. You might have a single customer or several customers or groups of customers, one or more internal suppliers or one or more external suppliers and all sorts of combinations of these. The Project Board will have to take the different interests in the project into account as regards its composition and decision-making. If one or more interests is insufficiently protected in a project, the involvement of the group concerned will come under pressure and the chance of the project failing will increase.

4.2.3 Project Board

The Project Board - consists of the Executive, the Senior User and the Senior Supplier and is the decision-making body for the project. The management level of the Project Board members is highly dependent on the sort, type and size of the project. However, it is important that each of the members has real authority to decide for the group he represents. It must not be the case that the Project Board takes decisions that continually have to be confirmed by a higher level of management. The Project Board must be able to make decisions and implement them personally.

The Project Board is appointed by line management or by programme management. The Project Board will be judged on the success of the project and is responsible for the project within the boundaries set by the line or programme management. It must guarantee that the project stays within the agreed tolerance levels and delivers the products according to the agreed specifications and quality, as described in the PID. The Project Board is also responsible for communication with the outside world.

In addition to the Project Board, all sorts of advisory bodies can be set up in projects, taken from the various stakeholder groups. However, these advisory bodies have no decision-making powers. They are a way of increasing involvement and managing expectations better.

The Executive - carries final responsibility for the project. This responsibility means that the Executive takes the ultimate decisions in the project. The Executive chairs the Project Board and is the owner of the Business Case. He is supported in this by the Senior User and the Senior Supplier. The Executive must ensure that the project delivers 'value for money' and that the aims stated in the Business Case can be achieved with the outcome of the project. In so doing, the

Executive must seek to maintain a balance between the interests of the customer, the users and the suppliers.

Furthermore, the Executive is responsible for setting up a good project organisation and a good creation of a plan. This means that the Executive must be heavily involved in the start-up stage and initiation stage of the project. Throughout the project, the Executive will be involved in possible issues and problems on a strategic level. He is responsible for taking the decisions on these and for communicating or escalating them to higher corporate or programme management. It is the Executive who formally closes the project and discharges the Project Manager. Finally, the Executive will chair the post-project review and communicate the outcome to the stakeholders. There is always only one Executive on a Project Board.

The Senior User - represents the interests of the users. The Senior User is responsible for the specifications, and their acceptance and quality criteria, being written fully and unambiguously, and for the product being fit for use. Representing the users, the Senior User is responsible for having the products tested where and whenever required, and will also have to indicate which of the users should be involved in these tests. The Senior User is furthermore responsible for the communication with the users or their management and for the commitment of people and resources from the users, should this be necessary for the project (for example, for writing specifications or for reviews). In the event of conflicting users' interests, the Senior User will have to take the final decision in respect of the project. He is responsible for approving Requests for Change from the users' point of view. The Senior User is often appointed as Change Authority on the Project Board. More than one person on a Project Board can fill the role of Senior User.

The Senior Supplier - represents the interests of those who design, acquire, develop and implement the actual project outcome. The Senior Supplier is responsible for the specialist products being produced within the criteria agreed. The Senior Supplier is responsible for the check on technical feasibility at the time the product is specified. In addition to this, the Senior Supplier contributes towards the designing of a plan and estimating of costs, and he is responsible for releasing sufficient resources to produce the project outcome according to specifications, within budget and according to plan. More than one person on a Project Board can fill the role of Senior Supplier.

Project Board in a customer-supplier relationship
As well as the Project Board for the project, there can also be platforms within the customer environment and within the supplier environment for discussing confidential matters concerning the project, without other parties being present. On the customer's platform, consultations will take place particularly concerning the user's wishes and requirements of the within the framework of the Business Case.

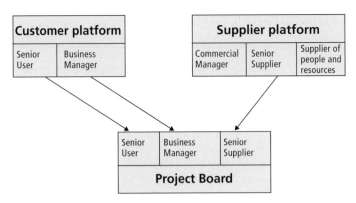

Figure 4.4 Project Board in a customer-supplier relationship

On the supplier's platform discussions will have to take place between the Senior Supplier, the management responsible for producing the specialist products and the management with commercial responsibility. The required commitment of people and the resources for the project will have to be determined and agreed in advance so that the Senior Supplier in the project can take on his responsibilities. If there is an external supplier, the Senior Supplier is often the supplier's account manager for this customer or project.

Project Assurance

Every member of the Project Board is responsible for the work in the project being carried out according to the agreements. This responsibility is called Project Assurance. This supervisory responsibility often takes up a great deal of time and requires specific qualities. Because the Project Board members do not usually have this time or these qualities, this task (entirely in line with the concept of 'management by exception') is often delegated to third parties. On behalf of the individual Project Board members, these third parties, Project Assurance, have the job of ensuring that all the work carried out in the project and by the Project Manager is done according to the fixed agreements. Project Assurance must also ensure that the Project Board receives the correct information. This role cannot be combined with that of Project Manager. Project Assurance reports directly to the Project Board.

The role of **Executive** in Project Assurance is to guarantee that:
• Costs and progress continue in line with those included in the approved Project Plan.
• The business risks are properly managed.
• The project continues in line with corporate or programme strategy and the Business Case therefore remains valid.
• The project's payments match the progress of the work so that financing the project is not endangered.

The role of Project Assurance for the Executive is usually played by one of the customer's Financial Controllers.

The role of **Senior User** in Project Assurance is to guarantee that:
• The users' quality expectations and Acceptance Criteria are correct, complete and unambiguous.
• From the users' point of view the products are tested sufficiently and various intervals in the project.

- Quality assessment procedures are observed from the users' point of view.
- The users' interests are safeguarded when changes are made.
- The users are represented by the right people in the quality reviews.
- Users' risks are managed sufficiently and that proper communication takes place with the users.

The role of Project Assurance for the Senior User is usually played by the customer's quality manager.

The role of **Senior Supplier** in Project Assurance is to guarantee that:
- A correct approach is chosen for the design and the development.
- Design and development standards are used correctly and effectively.
- The scope of the project does not expand imperceptibly.
- Quality assessment procedures are observed from the supplier's point of view.
- The interests of the suppliers are safeguarded when changes are made.
- The suppliers are represented by the right people in the quality reviews and suppliers' risks are managed sufficiently.

The supplier's quality manager usually plays the role of Project Assurance for the Senior Supplier.

4.2.4 Other roles in the Project Management Team

The Project Manager - is responsible for the day-to-day direction of the project on behalf of the Project Board and has the power to make decisions within the tolerance levels agreed with the Project Board. His primary responsibility is to ensure that the project delivers the agreed products, according to the agreed quality and within the agreed time and budget. In so doing, he must not lose sight of the fact that the delivery of the outcome is not an end in itself, but that the project objective must be achieved with the delivered outcome. The Project Manager is not responsible for this, but should remain vigilant as to whether achieving the Business Case is still realistic. He has the duty to report any risks of not achieving the Business Case to the Project Board. In so doing, he ought to come up with a solution with alternatives, where possible, and give advice.

The Team Manager - is responsible for producing the specialist products. The role of Team Manager is optional. The Project Manager may decide to direct the work himself. Team Managers are responsible for the MP process and, with this, for producing one or more specialist products according to an agreed Work Package. This Work Package contains the agreements about which outcome should be delivered according to which specifications and within which plan and budget. This is determined by the Project Manager based on the authorised Stage Plan and is accepted by the Team Manager.

Project Support - the Project Manager and the Team Managers often need support in the project not only due to the amount of work but also because there is specific expertise needed for planning, budgeting, configuration management etc. This support is called Project Support. The Project Manager directs the Project Support.

Project Support Office - in an environment in which several projects are being carried out at the same time, a separate Project Support Office may be set up. This office provides project support to all projects. A Project Support Office can be an extremely effective entity for supporting projects efficiently in an organisation. A Project Support Office is also often a good breeding ground for prospective Project Managers.

The Configuration Manager - is responsible for managing the products in an organisation, including a project organisation. Configuration Management is essential in projects for managing the project. The Configuration Manager is often part of Project Support. The Configuration Manager usually gets all the operational jobs in change control too. The Project Manager, however, is ultimately responsible for configuration management.

Combination of roles
Project Support, the Configuration Manager and the Team Managers are optional roles in a Project Management Team. All the other roles are mandatory within the PRINCE2 methodology. In exceptional cases, the role of the Executive and that of the Senior User or the role of the Executive and that of the Senior Supplier can be combined. The principle of the customer-supplier relationship does not permit the role of Senior User to be combined with that of Senior Supplier. If the nature of the activities makes such a combination possible, the work is a job in the line organisation and not a project.

4.3 Plans
Plans are documents describing who has to do what, where and when to achieve the intended result or objective and how that result has to be reached.

A good plan makes it clear whether the proposed objectives can be achieved within the given preconditions, lists the actions that have to be carried out to achieve thee objectives and indicates the required people and resources and the duration time of the plan.

4.3.1 Advantages of designing a plan
Designing a plan forces the stakeholders to think in advance about what has to be delivered in which order and what has to be done to achieve this. A good plan can ensure that there is agreement about how to tackle the execution. A good, transparent plan is a simple way of creating a support base among the stakeholders. Everyone gets a clear idea of what his individual contribution has to be to implement the plan. It also becomes clear what the mutual dependencies are between the various parties and between the planning activities and activities of third parties. When carrying out the work, the plan is a basis for evaluating the progress of the project.

4.3.2 Elements of a plan
A plan contains not only a schedule but also all the elements needed to achieve the aims that have been set. Which products have to be produced and in which order do they have to be produced? What has to be available or ready before a start is made on implementing the plan? Which actions are needed to produce the various deliverables? What are the dependencies between these actions? What is the required commitment of people and resources in order to carry out this work? Which dependencies with other projects and/or events are there? Which assumptions form the basis for implementing the plan (these could, for example, be assumptions about productivity or assumptions about dependencies)? What is the required budget for implementing the plan and how should the budget be distributed over the various items? What are the tolerance levels with respect to the aspects of time and money to implement the plan? Which quality controls have to be performed to be certain that the deliverables meet the quality requirements? And how much time, how many people and resources are need for this?

A plan provides an opportunity for analysing the risks at an early stage and to anticipate them. The planning stage can also be used to consider any alternatives if certain risks do materialise. Such alternatives can be included in the plan as a backup provision (contingency plans) and an item called 'contingency budget' can be included in the budget. Finally, a plan can include a budget for changes, as a reserve for future changes.

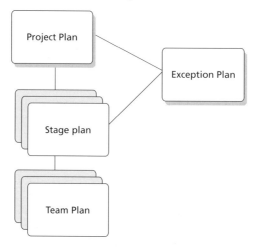

Figure 4.5 PRINCE2 plan levels (Based on: OGC source)

A plan forms the basis for the Project Manager or Team Manager for carrying out their own work and the work of their team. A plan is also the basis for obtaining authorisation for doing this work.

4.3.3 Plan approach
Designing a plan is an iterative process: it develops and gathers more detail on the way. Often there will be several people working on a plan, each one working on one or more parts of the plan. This makes exchanging information and looking together at the consequences for other parts of the plan on a very regular basis absolutely vital. Consultation with the Executive is important too, to ensure that the plan remains in line with the Executive's aims. This is the responsibility of the Project Manager.

Another important issue is to discuss the plan with the people and parties who will actually be doing the work, and to discuss it with the management that has to make the required people and resources available for the plan to be implemented. Involving these parties will increase the quality of the plan since the parties can provide qualified input about productivity, dependencies, etc. Involving these parties also increases their commitment and the support base from these parties that is necessary to be able to implement the plan.

4.3.4 Plan levels
PRINCE2 identifies three plan levels: the Project Plan, the Stage Plan and the Team Plan. Each plan level must match the needs of the relevant management level and must be in line with the higher-level plan. The lower the level of the plan, the shorter the duration time, but the more details the plan will contain.

4.3.5 Project Plan

The Project Plan is part of the PID and describes the entire project. The Project Plan is regarded as essential. The Project Plan contains a summary of all the important products with their necessary resources, the total cost and specific checkpoints, the management stages and which products have to be delivered in which stage. This makes it possible for the Project Board to direct the project throughout all its stages.

When the Project Board approves the PID, the initial Project Plan is fixed. This means that, even if changes are made, there is always a document showing the underlying principles on which the project was based at the start.

At the end of each stage, progress will be measured against the current Project Plan. Any adjustments will be incorporated into successive versions of the Project Plan.

4.3.6 Stage Plan

The Stage Plan is the Project Manager's working document for that specific stage. A Stage Plan must be written for each stage in a project. The Stage Plan is a detailed plan showing the approach to be taken for that specific stage. The same elements appear in the Stage Plan as are included in the Project Plan, but they now contain much more detail and are only for the relevant stage, plus the work data the Project Manager needs for the day-to-day management of that stage. These could be, for example, the relevant reporting and meeting dates and the various dates on which the reviews and tests of the products are planned. These dates are not usually specified explicitly in the Project Plan.

If the project only has one execution stage, it is often a good idea to physically include the Stage Plan detail within the Project Plan.
The Stage Plan enables the Project Manager to steer the project in the right direction and manage it on a day-to-day basis, even if external parties are doing part of the work.

Designing the Stage Plan takes place in the last period of the previous stage. In other words, before the Project Board has given its approval to start that stage. This process is described in more detail in section 3.7, Managing Stage Boundaries (SB).

4.3.7 Team Plan

If it is necessary to work out a Work Package in more detail in a project, a team plan can be designed. The team plan is an optional plan and therefore not compulsory. The team plan is intended to enable Team Managers to manage a Work Package or several Work Packages in a specialist team or supplier.

In general, an external supplier will make its own team plan. Nonetheless, the work carried out remains the responsibility of the Project Manager. The supplier's plan will have to fit in with the Project Manager's Stage Plan and all this has to be in line with the contract concluded between the Executive and the supplier.

4.3.8 Exception Plan

In addition to these three plans, PRINCE2 also has the Exception Plan. The Exception Plan replaces the Stage and/or Project Plan that is threatening to exceed the tolerance.

If the Stage and/or Project Plan are threatening to exceed the agreed tolerance levels, the Project Manager will first report this to the Project Board by means of an Exception Report. Based on this Exception Report, the Project Board will give the Project Manager instructions for bringing the stage and/or project back on course. The Project Manager will then use these instructions to draw up the Exception Plan.

The Exception Plan has the same structure as the plan it replaces, with the only extra feature being that a copy of the Exception Report is included as a reference in the Exception Plan. The Project Board should be able to base its decision on whether the project is to continue or be stopped on the Exception Plan. When making provisions for project tolerance levels being exceeded the Project Board will have to seek the approval of line or programme management.

4.4 Controls

Control has everything to do with decision-making and is crucial for project management. The project has to be controlled to guarantee that the desired result is delivered on time and within budget and that there is always a valid Business Case for carrying out the project.

Control comprises all the directive and regulatory activities that aim at allowing all the specialist activities to run according to plan. In contrast to the specialist activities, control is a continuous process. Control happens in a loop, as it were, of planning, recording, evaluating and adjusting (see figure 4.6).

Figure 4.6 Control circle

Control provides a guarantee that every level of the Project Management Team (Team Manager, Project Manager, Project Board) can evaluate progress, compare the results produced with the planned results, test follow-on plans and options on the basis of various scenarios, detect problems, take corrective measures and authorise follow-on actions.

4.4.1 Management by exception

PRINCE2 employs the concept of 'management by exception' for senior management to control the project. This implies that the Project Manager only reports to the Project Board members, if that is considered necessary or desirable from a management point of view. What is more, these reports focus on management issues within the framework of the defined Business Case. This prevents senior management from having to concern itself frequently with the progress of the project.

To have the project directed properly, the senior management of the customer's organisation must also take the lead in the project and have a seat on the Project Board. However, senior management hardly has time for this and often pulls out during the project, or right from the start leaves the directing to lower or middle management in the organisation. It does not help to increase their involvement by seeking to involve them more and more intensively in the project. That only leads to an even greater claim on their limited time. Management by exception is the only practical approach: decision-making only if it is necessary from a management point of view and only on aspects that are relevant from a business point of view. Throughout the project, only short management reports are presented to keep senior management up-to-date on the progress of the project.

In the initiation stage the Project Manager, in consultation with the Project Board, determines the essential decision-making points to be planned in for the Project Board. The project is thus divided up into what are known as management stages.

At management stage boundaries, the Project Board will take a no go/go decision as to whether the project is to be continued and, if so, in which form. This is also the moment when the Project Manager is discharged from responsibility for the previous stage, the Stage Plan for the next stage is approved, the people and resources required to implement the next Stage Plan are released and the Project Manager is given authorisation to start the implementation of the next stage.

During the management stages the Project Manager is in charge of day-to-day management of the project and he works on the basis of the approved Stage Plan without intervention from, or mandatory consultations with, the Project Board. A decision is only required from the Project Board during a management stage if an exception to the plan threatens to take place. This exception will be related to the tolerance levels agreed in advance between the Project Board and the Project Manager. These tolerance levels are recorded in the Stage Plan.

4.4.2 Project Board controls
The most important Project Board controls in a project are:
- **The authorisation to start the Project Initiation** - are there sufficient reasons for starting a project and for authorising the activities for project initiation? This first decision point is also known as the 'decision to justify'. This is the official start of the project.
- **The authorisation to start implementing the project** - the Project Initiation and the subsequent decision to authorise the implementation of the project. This is also the moment when the customer usually releases the budget for the project. This second decision point is also known as the 'decision to fund'.
- **End stage assessment** - at the end of each management stage the Project Board has to decide whether there are still sufficient reasons for continuing with the project (no go/go): is the project on course, is there still a valid Business Case, has the work in the previous stage been completed satisfactorily and can we authorise the next stage and are the required people and resources available?
- **Highlight Report** - interim reports from the Project Manager to the Project Board to inform the Project Board members about the progress of the project.
- **Exception Report** - a report from the Project Manager to the Project Board if the Project Manager discovers that one or more tolerance levels in the Stage Plan and/or the Project Plan are in danger of being exceeded.
- **Exception assessment** - the Project Board meeting in which the Exception Plan at issue has to be assessed and approved.

- **Project closure** - the closing Project Board meeting in which the Project Board members must convince themselves that the project outcome has actually been delivered to the satisfaction of the various parties, that the follow-on actions have been identified and recorded, that a good evaluation of the project has taken place and that a plan has been drawn up for a post-project review.

To be able to control the project, attention should be paid to a controlled start, a controlled implementation and a controlled closure of the project.

4.4.3 Controlled start

All preparatory activities in the run up to the project and in the initiation stage are aimed at guaranteeing a planned execution of the specialist activities.

In the process Starting up a Project, these activities mainly involve organising the Project Management Team and writing the Project Brief, but also include planning the initiation stage. The Initiation Stage Plan guarantees a controlled implementation of the initiation stage, which is the basis for a controlled implementation of the rest of the project.

Based on the documents produced at the start of the project, the Project Board establishes whether there are sufficient reasons for starting the project (Decision to Justify) and if so, the Project Board then authorises the implementation of the initiation stage. This is an explicit no go/go decision. The Project Board must not give approval too lightly, but only if there is sufficient justification. This is the official start of the project.

In the initiation stage the Project Manager is responsible for the creation of the PID. The PID is the basis for gaining the approval of the Project Board for implementing the project and is also the basis for planned execution. Important elements of the PID are the Project Quality Plan, Project Plan, Business Case, Risk Log and agreements on how project control will be organised. The Project Plan, Business Case and Risk Log particularly have to be updated regularly throughout the project, at least at the end of every stage.

The initiation stage is also the time when the management stages are agreed and included in the Project Plan as part of the PID.

Finally, in the initiation stage the Communication Plan is drawn up to deal with communication to and from the project stakeholders. This plan records what information is needed by whom during the project, at what frequency and in which form the information should be presented. The Communication Plan is also part of the PID. Please refer to appendix 7.2.4 for the contents of the Communication Plan.

4.4.4 Controlled progress

Tolerance levels

An important control is the agreement between the various parties in the project management structure on tolerance levels. A tolerance is a permissible deviation from the agreed value without escalating the deviation to the next level of management. Tolerance levels are needed to take care of minor setbacks and necessary adjustments when carrying out the work.

Tolerance levels have to be agreed between corporate or programme management and the Project Board, between the Project Board and the Project Manager and between the Project Manager and the Team Manager in the Project Plan, the Stage Plans and the Work Packages respectively (see figure 4.7).

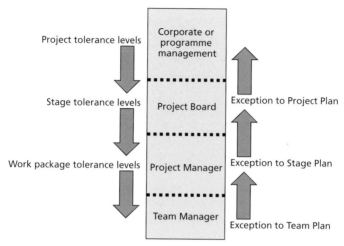

Figure 4.7 Agreements on tolerance levels between various levels of management (Source: OGC)

Tolerance levels in projects are traditionally agreed with particular reference to time and money, but agreements on tolerance levels in projects can also be made for quality, scope, benefits and risks:

- **Tolerance levels for quality** - this could include a desired functionality for a particular product that is not strictly necessary.
- **Tolerance levels for scope** - the scope of the project could be to deliver a number of modules where some modules are absolutely essential and others will only be delivered if there is enough time and/or budget.
- **Tolerance levels for benefits** - as long as the project achieves the intended result within certain boundaries, the Business Case will continue to be supported.
- **Tolerance levels for risks** - how much risk is the Project Board prepared to take? Depending on the situation, more risks may be able to be taken with regard to quality than with regard to time or money.

Tolerance levels in time and money must have an upper and lower limit. Delivering too early could lead to alignment problems with other projects. Information about budgets that are to be released must be made known in good time so that they can be used for other purposes.

Tolerance levels must not be confused with a change budget or a contingency budget. A tolerance is the 'freedom' a manager has with regard to the next level, to be able to correct plans where necessary. A change budget is a budget specifically allocated to a change authority to pay for approved changes. A contingency budget is a budget allocated to finance a previously specified contingency plan that needs to come into effect if a certain risk occurs.

> **Columbus' trick?**
>
> When Christopher Columbus crossed the Atlantic Ocean in search of new trading routes to India, he applied the principle of 'tolerance levels'.
>
> Instead of being at the ready 24 hours a day in case he needed to steer the ship, he made agreements with his helmsman. Together they determined the course to be followed. Columbus also gave his helmsman the freedom to adjust this course if he considered it necessary. They made agreements about permissible exceptions to the course. These were what we now call tolerance levels. By working in this way, Columbus was able to work on other things and get some well-earned sleep in the captain's cabin. Columbus and his helmsman also agreed that the helmsman would follow the course plotted without any further explanation or consultation. Only when the helmsman anticipated that, for whatever reason, he would be unable to follow the agreed course, would he ring the ship's bell. This was the sign for Columbus to go immediately to the helmsman to make a decision and possibly plot a new course, even in the middle of the night.

Product Descriptions

A Product Description contains all the essential information required to be able to make a specific product. A Product Description must be written as soon as it is known that a product is to be produced in the project. The Product Description must be frozen once the plan to produce the product has been established. The Product Description describes:

- Why a product is needed.
- The elements from which it is constituted.
- What materials or data the product is based upon.
- Who is responsible for production.
- Which requirements are placed on the product.
- That the product meets these requirements.
- How and by whom testing will be done.
- How the product is to be delivered to the customer.

Work Package

A Work Package is a collection of agreements needed to produce one or more, possibly specialised, products in a controlled manner. A Work Package contains:

- The Product Description.
- The start date and the time when the products have to be delivered.
- The budget available.
- The commitment of people and resources.
- The interfaces with other Work Packages or projects.
- Agreements about when the various quality checks have to be performed.
- How progress is to be reported and how the products are to be delivered.

A full list can be found in appendix 7.2.32. The Project Manager will assign the Work Package (CS1) to the Team Manager who must accept it (SB1). If a Work Package is simply 'thrown over the wall', the Team Manager can never take responsibility for the work to be done.

Quality Check

Carrying out the final quality checks is the ultimate test of whether the deliverables meet the quality requirements previously set for them. To control these checks properly, it is important to establish in advance which checks have to be made, when these checks are planned and who is to do these checks for all the products to be tested. To get a good overall view this information must be registered in a Quality Log. As soon as a quality check has taken place, the result and any actions to be taken must also be recorded in the Quality Log, with a reference to all the inspection documents that have to be filed.

The Project Manager is responsible for organising the Quality Log. The list of tests to be carried out will be drawn up for each stage when drawing up the Stage Plan (SB1). The Team Manager is responsible for the quality checks being done and for their results being recorded in the Quality Log (MP2). This status is important input for the Project Manager for monitoring the progress of the work (CS2).

Change Control

Change control is an essential control for the Project Manager. Projects are carried out in a changing environment and changes to a project cannot therefore be avoided. It is the responsibility of the Project Manager to ensure that changes are implemented in a controlled manner.

When implementing changes in a controlled manner, the Project Manager must ensure that, in the case of authorised changes, the relevant configuration record and the corresponding Product Description are also changed.

Risk Log

Organising and using the Risk Log is likewise an important control for the Project Manager. Care must be taken to prevent identified risks and countermeasures from escaping management's notice. The use of the Risk Log is a practical instrument for managing risks effectively in projects. See the component Risks.

Checkpoint Reports

These are the reports the Team Manager makes to the Project Manager about the progress of the work in an assigned Work Package. A Checkpoint Report is written at a set time, for example once a week or once every two weeks, and has a fixed layout (see appendix 7.2.3). The contents of and the intervals between reports will be agreed by the Project Manager and the Team Manager in the Work Package. The Checkpoint Report can be linked to the progress meetings between the Project Manager and his Team Managers. The Checkpoint Report is also a good medium for the Team Manager to inform the members of his team about the progress of the Work Package.

Plans

The Project Manager will have to continually plan the work that is to be carried out. The standard plans during the implementation of the project are the Stage Plans that are written as part of Managing Stage Boundaries (SB1). However, the Project Manager cannot usually avoid having to implement adjustments to the Stage Plan as part of Taking Corrective Action (CS7), to ensure that the activities in that stage are carried out within the agreed tolerance levels. The Team Manager makes a team plan to be able to accept the Work Package (MP1). This team plan will also have to be adjusted often during the implementation of the Work Package (MP2).

Highlight Report

The Project Manager writes a Highlight Report for the Project Board members at fixed times. The interval between reports will be agreed in advance in the initiation stage with the Project

Board members. The Highlight Report indicates:
- The current status.
- What has been achieved in the current period and what is planned for the coming period.
- The topical Project Issues and risks and any consequences.

The Highlight Report is an important part of the concept of management by exception. The Highlight Report confirms to the Project Board members that the project is progressing within the agreed tolerance levels.

End Stage Report
At the end of each stage (except at the very end of the project) the Project Manager will have to write an End Stage Report. The Project Manager writes the End Stage Report in the process SB5. The End Stage Report describes:
- The results of the current stage.
- The current state of affairs in the project.
- An update of the Project Plan, the Business Case and the risks.
- The state of affairs around the Project Issues and the quality assessments carried out.
- An account by the Project Manager of the performance in the stage just ended.

Using the End Stage Report as its base, the Project Board can accept from the Project Manager the results of the current stage.

End Stage Assessment
The End Stage Report, together with the completed current and planned next Stage Plans, the updated Project Plan and the current Risk Log, is the documentation based on which the Project Board has to take a no go/go decision on continuing the project. The Project Board must verify whether the previous stage was completed satisfactorily and according to agreements. The Project Board must assess and approve the Stage Plan and must ensure that the required people and resources are available for the Stage Plan. The Project Board must verify whether the agreed tolerance levels for the next stage are still correct or whether they should be adjusted. If all this is correct, the Project Board will be able to authorise the execution of the next stage. It is a realistic possibility that the Project Board will have to decide that there is no point in continuing the project. The Project Board will then instruct the Project Manager to close the project prematurely.

Exception Report
If the work in a stage is threatening to exceed the agreed tolerances, the Project Manager must escalate this to the Project Board. In so doing, the Project Manager must not only indicate the causes and consequences for the project, but also which solutions he envisages. You do not report problems, you report solutions. This can be done verbally, but it is often better to do it in writing. The Exception Report contains a structured layout for this report (see appendix 7.2.10).

Exception Assessment
Based on the Exception Report, the Project Board decides what needs to be done and what the best option is (DP4). The Project Board instructs the Project Manager to elaborate this option into a complete Exception Plan (SB). The Project Manager submits this Exception Report to the Project Board. The Assessment of the Exception Plan takes place in a special meeting of the Project Board in which the Project Board makes a definitive decision as to whether and how the project should be continued (DP3). It remains a realistic possibility that the Project Board has to decide that there is no longer any point in continuing with the project. The Project Board will

then instruct the Project Manager to close the project prematurely (CP). Another valid action by the Project Board is to remove the cause of the tolerance deviation and allow the Project Manager to continue with the current Stage Plan. An example here might be a decision by the Project Board to delay implementation of a change request that is causing the deviation until after the current project is finished.

Daily Log

A Daily Log can be a useful tool for both the Project Manager and a Team Manager to help them manage their work. All sorts of notes can be included in the log, such as:
- Notes of telephone calls and meetings that do not all have to be formally confirmed, but which do involve agreements, some of them important.
- Own action points from meetings so that he can take action before the minutes of the meeting are distributed.
- Receipt and dispatch of goods, etc.

4.4.5 Controlled closure

Before a project can be closed the following must be guaranteed:
- That the project outcome has been delivered according to the agreement and satisfaction of all parties.
- That the maintenance and support for the outcome has been arranged.
- That a good evaluation of lessons learned has taken place.
- That any follow-on actions have been identified and recorded.
- That a plan is drawn up to measure, as soon as this is possible, whether the intended benefits the customer wanted from the outcome will be achieved.

The supporting documents for the controlled closure are:
- **Project Closure Notification** - the Project Closure Recommendation from the Project Manager to the Project Board members followed by the official Project Closure Notification from the Project Board to all parties who supply people, resources and services to the project being closed. This should make it possible to disband the project team and dismantle the facilities in a controlled manner.
- **Delivery Protocols** - the project outcome must be delivered to the organisation that will be given the practical responsibility for maintaining and managing the outcome. Both the people in the organisation who are responsible for the ultimate support and maintenance and the people and the organisation that will ultimately be using the outcome have to accept the final outcome. These acceptances must be recorded explicitly in what are called delivery protocols. Any unresolved points must be recorded with them. This should include transfer of the project's Configuration Item Records to the configuration management system of those who will maintain the outcome.
- **End Project Report** - this is a similar report to the End Stage Report, but now for the whole project. This report shows the following:
  - The final outcome delivered.
  - Expenses incurred and course of the project.
  - A summary of the Project Issues.
  - A summary of the approved changes and their impact on the project and Business Case and the quality assessments carried out.
  - An account by the Project Manager of how the project has gone and the data and the agreements made with respect to the post-project review still to be held.

The Project Manager should not write this report to the Project Board but for the Project Board. The Project Board members must be able to use the report to account for the project in their own organisations.

- **Follow-on Action Recommendations** - this includes all outstanding actions that still have to be carried out after the project. The Issue Log is an important basis for preparing follow-on actions. Requests for Change at the end of the project are often not actioned within the project because they might cause the project to be in danger of running out of time and/or budget. The Executive often shifts these actions on to later enhancement projects. If these actions are not properly recorded and handed over, users, maintenance and support may be faced with problems.

- **Lessons Learned Report** - the Lessons Learned Report contains the results of the lessons learned evaluation at the end of the project. Good use can be made here of the lessons learned that have been recorded throughout the project in the Lessons Learned Log. It must be appreciated that the lessons learned in the Lessons Learned Log are intended in the first place for improvements in the project team. The lessons learned in the Lessons Learned Report are intended mainly to be lessons learned for the customer and supplier organisations involved. What often happens is that separate Lessons Learned Reports are prepared for the separate organisations.

- **Post-Project Review Plan** - the benefits from the deliverables can often only be actually measured after some time. This evaluation is recorded in the Post-Project Review Plan. The implementation of this plan falls outside the scope of the project.

4.4.6 Stages

A stage is a segmentation of the project in time, with previously defined activities and deliverables. We make a distinction between two stage types: management stages and technical stages.

Management stages

Management stages are subdivisions of the project in time, linked to a no go/go decision with respect to continuing the project. There is a direct dependence with the allocation of people, resources and authority. These previously agreed decision points take place at the end of each management stage. The management stages are arranged sequentially.

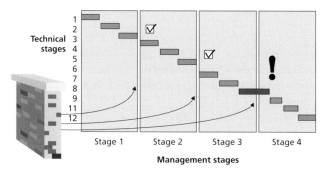

Figure 4.8 Management stages

There are always at least two management stages in a project: the (mandatory) initiation stage in which the PID is created, and an implementation stage for developing the deliverables. Implementation can be divided into several stages.

The current management stage comprises all the work released by the Project Board and that will be carried out by the Project Manager on the instructions of the Project Board. If no management stages are defined, there is a risk that the project is driven by specialist teams instead of by the Project Board. Management stages enable the Project Board members to drive the project directly. What is the current position of the project? Can the project still be carried out in technical terms? Is there still a Business Case for continuing the project? What are the risks and how can we assess them in the light of the goals to be achieved? Management stages are an important aspect of the principle we recommend of management by exception.

Dividing a project up into management stages gives the project management the opportunity of planning the project in outline based on the Project Plan and of specifying the work at hand in more detail. At each stage boundary, the Project Plan is then updated and a new detailed plan is drawn up for the next stage. This is also called the 'rolling wave' principle.

Before the Project Board gives a 'go' for execution of the next stage, the Project Board must approve the Stage Plan for the next stage and it must also confirm the required commitment of people and resources. It is therefore a good idea to plan management stage boundaries immediately before the commitment of important/new resources is required or before the project has to take substantial risks in the implementation of the project.

When dividing the implementation up into several management stages, account must be taken of the extent to which the project work can be planned in advance. Furthermore, it is a good idea to have the management stages tailored to critical decision points in the project. These may be internal decision points, but may also be external decision points: the introduction of a new product, the approval of the business plan, choices, etc. Moreover, it is recommended that the management stages be spread fairly evenly over the implementation process. Having a lot of short stages next to a few long ones is not a very good idea.

A management stage boundary creates the opportunity to change the people in the Project Management Team. This is obviously not something to be preferred, but is often unavoidable in lengthy projects. For example, different skills for Project Assurance may be needed in the next stage. Dividing the project into management stages is also conducive to team motivation. Many people find it difficult to tackle aims that lie well in the future. A shorter time scale can considerably improve team motivation.

Technical stages

Technical stages are characterised by the application of specialist knowledge and skills, for example when making a rough design, a detailed design, building, testing and implementing. The number of technical stages is often greater than the number of management stages. In contrast to management stages, various technical stages can run in parallel so that several products can be developed more quickly.

A practical point for attention arises when a technical stage 'cuts across' various management stages. After all, at the end of a management stage, a no go/go decision has to be taken. The activities in a technical stage thus have to be arranged in such a way that the products to be developed can be clearly assigned to separate management stages.

4.5 Management of Risk

Risk is defined in the Netherlands Competence Baseline (NCB) as:

> *The chance that a fact or circumstance will occur in the future and the consequences it will have for the project.*

Another modern definition of risk is 'uncertainty about the outcome'. This can be both negative and positive. Risks can also create an opportunity and should be managed as such. In everyday use, risks are mainly associated with threats. In this chapter we assume this more usual definition of risk.

4.5.1 Conditions for management of risk

Every project has its risks and this cannot be avoided. Waiting until there is not a single risk forming a threat to the project is not an option. The success of a project lies in managing the risks and, with this, limiting the unplanned consequences for the project to an acceptable minimum. This can be done in a number of ways. It is important to understand that the management of risk is a continuous activity. It is not something that takes place only at the beginning of a project and is never looked at again. Management of risk is a job for the Project Manager, but all those working on the project also have a role to play. To be able to apply management of risk well in a project, a number of things are vital:

- Reliable and up-to-date information.
- Decision-making on the basis of thorough risk analyses.
- Management mechanisms to check risks.
- Balance between risks and countermeasures.

In addition, it is important that the Project Board is behind the idea of management of risk and actively promotes it. To do so, the Project Board must make sufficient capacity available to be able to carry out the agreed measures. All participants in the project must be aware of the management of risk approach. A standardised approach to management of risk can make a contribution.

4.5.2 Risk tolerance

It is essential that, at the beginning of the project, the Project Board and the Project Manager make agreements about the risks that are acceptable. These can be different depending on what the risk relates to. Risks that have consequences for the delivery may be far less acceptable than risks that have consequences for the budget, or the other way round. The extent to which a risk is acceptable to management is called the risk tolerance. It is possible that during the course of the project, 'flexibility' occurs in what is acceptable and what is not. It is important that the Project Manager comes to agreements with the Project Board on this and develops a feeling for what the risk tolerance is for the Project Board.

4.5.3 Responsibilities

The Project Manager is responsible for identifying and recording the risks, for conducting risk analyses and for incorporating risk measures into the plans. The Executive in the Project Board is the person ultimately responsibility for management of risk in the project.

The Project Board must inform the Project Manager of risks from outside the project. In addition, it must ultimately decide on the countermeasures to be taken. The Project Manager will submit one or more countermeasures with a recommendation, but it is the Project Board that ultimately decides. The Project Board decides on the countermeasures to be taken and, in so doing, must find a balance between the cost of the risk measures and the management of risk. This is where the considerable dependency between risks and the Business Case comes into play.

When considering risks that also have an impact on the programme or corporate organisation, the Project Board is also responsible for communicating with these organisations. When the project is in a programme, it is certainly important that the management of risk in the project is tailored to the management of risk for the programme.

4.5.4 Risk owner
The risk owner is responsible for monitoring a specific risk. A risk owner must be appointed for every risk. This will be the person who is best placed to detect whether a risk is increasing, decreasing or whether the threat is actually becoming a reality. The Project Manager will present the Project Board with a proposal as to who should be the owner of which risk. The Project Board takes the decision. Project Board members may also be appointed as owners, certainly if risks from outside the project are involved. The Executive is the risk owner of the risks that directly affect the Business Case.

4.5.5 Management of risk cycle
The world is continually changing and so too the project world and all the risks that go with it. The proposition that the project should be made independent if its environment has been advanced many times in the past, but this does not work. This introduces a far greater risk, namely that a project starts to take on a life of its own and in the end deviates further and further from the Executive's aim and from the requirements and wishes of the users. But what is the solution?

It is important to realise that things always change and that management of risk is a continuous process. Management of risk can be shown as a cyclical process. See figure 4.9. The cycle can be further subdivided into risk analysis and management of risk itself. Risk analysis comprises identifying and assessing the risks and identifying and selecting appropriate countermeasures. Management of risk consists of planning and allocating these countermeasures and monitoring and reporting on the further development of the risks. The results of the risk analysis and the management of risk are recorded in the Risk Log (see appendix 7.2.30).

The Project Manager will have to periodically evaluate the identified risks and where necessary take corrective measures (the 'filled in' arrows in figure 4.9). In preparation for the decisions of the Project Board and in the case of new Project Issues and escalations and when drawing up plans, the Project Manager will have to carry out a new risk analysis over and over again. (The shaded arrow in figure 4.9)

4.5.6 Risk analysis

Identifying risks
Identifying risks is a creative process and will lead to a list of possible risks for the project. This can be done, for example, by sitting down with a group of people and brainstorming until a list is produced. This is often an excellent option, but sometimes a project is so complex or extensive that it is better to split the project up and then identify the risks for each part. After that one will have to look at the risks that span several or all parts.

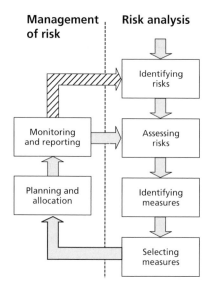

Figure 4.9 Management of a risk cycle (Based on: OGC source)

When identifying risks it can help to make a list of risk categories. A distinction can be made between strategic/commercial, economic/financial, legal, organisational, political, environmental and technical risks. It is important to realise that when identifying risks one must look further than simply the internal project risks. The risks to the project and for achieving the Business Case from outside are often just as important to the Executive as the internal risks. In addition, it may be that the identified risks are not in themselves damaging, but a combination may be fatal for the project. It is a good idea to look at all the factors that could stop the project from achieving the aims of the Business Case with as open a mind as possible.

When identifying risks, not only must the risk be described, but also the effect it may have on the project. The same threat can have more than one effect on the project, each having a different impact on the project's success and each needing to be addressed in a different way.

Breakdown en route

As a risk, a breakdown is not identified specifically enough. A breakdown that requires the roadside service to be called out is one thing, a breakdown involving your engine blowing up is quite another. Both instances of a breakdown en route have to be considered as different risks. Each of these risks is perceived by those involved in different ways. It would not be the first time that parties are talking at cross-purposes because the one imagines a simple breakdown, while the other envisages the whole engine blowing up.

Besides the effect risk has on the project, the risk category and the possible risk owner must also be shown for each risk when identifying the risks. The risk, the effect of the risk, the risk category and the risk owner are recorded in the Risk Log.

Evaluating risks

The identified risks are explained one by one during the evaluation. The chance of each risk occurring is determined as well as the impact the risk will have on the success of the project, and when the risk will occur. Multiplying the chance by the impact leads to a risk profile.

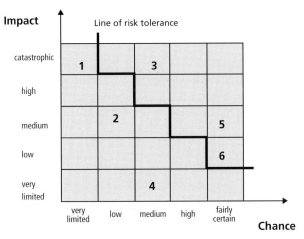

Figure 4.10 Risk profile (Based on: OGC source)

The chance that a risk occurs can be expressed in different ways. One can choose to express the chance in terms like very limited, low, medium, high and fairly certain or in figures, for example 1 through 5. A more precise subdivision often only gives a false certainty.

When carrying out the impact analysis, one must examine the consequences of a risk for the project not only in terms of time, money, quality, scope, safety, resources, etc., but also with respect to the benefits to be achieved.

The risk period is important for being able to set priorities properly (which risks should receive attention first). The risk period is expressed in time (for example, months, weeks or days).
A risk profile is drawn up to be able to compare the chance and impact values of the various risks in the form of a graph (see figure 4.10).

Identifying suitable measures
A distinction can be made between roughly five different measures:
- **Prevention** - the countermeasure prevents the risk from occurring.
- **Reduction** - the impact and/or the chance of the risk is reduced.
- **Transfer** - the risk is placed with another party, for example with a supplier or an insurer.
- **Preparing a contingency plan** - when the risk occurs, this plan takes effect.
- **Acceptance** - taking the risk is acceptable for the project or no affordable countermeasure is possible.

It is advisable to define several countermeasures for each risk.

Selecting measures
When selecting the measures, the chance and the impact of the risk are set against the cost and the possible consequences of the possible countermeasures. Besides the cost, the impact of the measures on other activities and the possible profits have to be looked at, not forgetting whether the countermeasures themselves do not introduce new risks.

4.5.7 Management of risk

Planning and allocation

The measures decided upon usually have to be worked out first in more detail. Who exactly is going to take which action and when, and what is the required commitment of people and resources? Once all this has been worked out, the measures can be included in the Project Plan and the respective Stage Plans, or can be designated as activities to be carried out immediately or as a contingency plan. Then the measures taken can be examined to see whether they still fit the context of the plans at hand. Finally, the Project Board definitively approves and authorises the measures for implementation as being part of the Project Plan or Stage Plan in question.

Monitoring and reporting

Monitoring and reporting the countermeasures are part of normal project management. The measures are included in the regular plans and are also reported as part of the monitoring of the regular plans. Monitoring and reporting as part of management of risk relate to the monitoring and reporting of the risks to be managed. Have the measures taken had the desired effect on the risk? If so, how will the risk develop in time? Will the chance and/or the possible impact of the risk increase again during the course of the project? Will new risks emerge that were not previously anticipated? And finally, are we as a Project Management Team sufficiently alert to risks and is our management of risk process effective?

4.5.8 Management of risk in processes

The management of risk is a continuous process and may not be viewed separately from the day-to-day management of the project. The management of risk is certainly not a once-only event.

In the start up process (SU4), in the initiation stage (IP3), at every stage end (SB4), when Work Packages are authorised (CS1), when Project Issues are analysed (CS4) and when an Exception Report is prepared (CS8) the Project Manager must carry out a new risk analysis. The Team Manager must analyse the risks when taking on Work Packages (MP1). Every time a plan is drawn up it will have to be examined whether risk measures have to be included in the plan (PL3). Before a plan can be completed, the consequences the plan may have on the identified risks will have to be examined as well as whether the plan means that new risks are introduced. (PL6).

The Project Manager will have to periodically evaluate the identified risks in the stage (CS5) and, where necessary, take corrective action (CS7). The Project Manager periodically reports on the status of the risks in the stage in the Highlight Report (CS6). At stage boundaries, the Project Manager reports to the Project Board on the risks in the End Stage Report (SB5). Identified risks for the operational use of the outcome are input for the Follow-on Action Recommendations (CP2). Risks and risk measures are an important item on the agenda of every meeting with the Project Board (DP1-5).

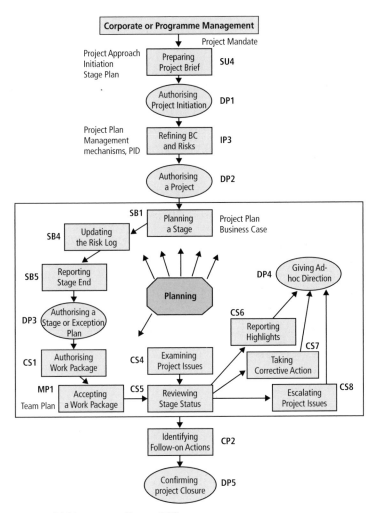

Figure 4.11 Management of risk in processes (Source: OGC)

4.6 Quality

Quality is defined in the ISO 8402 as:

> *The extent to which the totality of characteristics of a product bears on its ability to satisfy stated and implied needs.*

4.6.1 Quality management

To ensure that the customer's quality expectations are met, it is necessary to guarantee the desired quality by means of a quality management system. The purpose of a quality management system is to bring the 'expectation' and 'experience' of quality into line.

Suppose, for example, that the customer's perception of quality (experience) is less or lower than his expectation. He will then talk about 'poor' quality.

Strangely enough, the opposite is true too. If the quality perception is higher than expected, the customer may think that too many resources have been expended to achieve that level of quality. Resources that probably could have been 'better' spent. A practical attitude towards work in projects is therefore: 'best is the enemy of good'. Perfectionism may produce better products but costs more resources and in projects these are scarce.

The quality system must ensure that 'everything goes right first time' and that ultimately the products the customer has asked for are delivered. The quality system comprises a series of cohesive processes, procedures and responsibilities for implementing this quality management. For example, rules must be established for how goods are to be purchased: may the Project Manager or Team Manager do this himself or is this reserved for a qualified purchase department? Should use be made of 'preferred suppliers'? Who may/must sign for this?

Quality assurance

A project can make use of its own quality system, but can also use the customer's or the supplier's quality system. The Project Manager is responsible within his project for the organisation and maintenance of the project quality system. For their part, the customer's quality manager and the supplier's quality manager have to see to it that the quality system is properly organised and applied in the project. When carrying out interim evaluations to check whether the project is working according to the quality system and whether the quality processes and procedures are appropriate for the needs of the current project, the Project Manager can make use of the quality staff in the standing organisations.

Quality planning

Quality is often something that is imposed on people working a project. Although management keeps a tight rein on time and money, there is often scant attention paid to quality, except when it is too late and products are rejected. This often happens because, during preparations for the project, insufficient attention has been given to the processes and procedures to be used and because hardly any time, people or resources are reserved to guarantee quality and to really evaluate the various interim products. It is therefore of crucial importance for a project that quality is planned early on in the project. Not only must be quality requirements be laid down in the initiation stage, but also the quality system to be used and how the eventual interim and final products are to be tested. All this must be recorded in the Project Quality Plan that forms part of the PID. After that, the checks/tests to be performed in each stage have to be recorded in the relevant Stage Plan and the required commitment of people and resources to be reserved. By recording this explicitly in the stage quality plan, quality management should be saved from falling between two stools when it comes to the final stage planning.

Quality control

Quality control comprises the final checks on the (interim) products in the project. These serve to demonstrate that the deliverables meet the quality requirements for the products as set in advance.

4.6.2 The PRINCE2 quality path

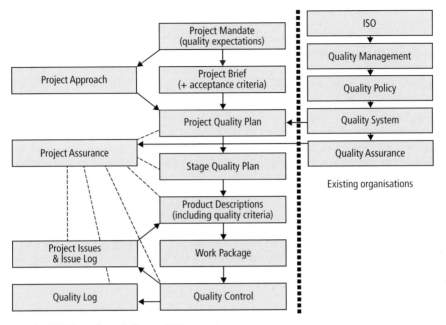

Figure 4.12 The PRINCE2 quality path (Source: OGC)

The quality in a project is guaranteed in the PRINCE2 method by:
- The attention paid to the customer's quality expectations and Acceptance Criteria.
- The quality planning.
- The activities aimed at quality assurance in the processes.
- The attention paid to configuration management and change control.
- The involvement of users and specialists early on in the project.

The PRINCE2 quality approach starts with specifying the customer's most important quality expectations in the Project Mandate. The process Starting Up a Project includes discussions with the various stakeholders in the customer's organisation in which the most important Acceptance Criteria for the deliverables are established. These are recorded in the Project Brief and form an important basis for the later project initiation.

Quality expectations influence the decision on how the project will be implemented and vice versa. When designing the project management structure for the project organisation, specifications are laid down for project assurance and with that, who is responsible for quality assurance in the project on behalf of the organisations involved. Often use is made of staff from the quality departments of the standing organisations for this.

The Project Brief, the Project Approach and the quality system provided by the standing organisations form the basis for drawing up the Project Quality Plan. The quality expectations and Acceptance Criteria in the Project Brief form the input for drawing up the quality requirements for the individual deliverables in the project. The customer's quality systems and those of the supplier are input for the project quality system. The Project Approach provides direction for both the Acceptance Criteria and the quality processes and procedures to be used. The Project Quality Plan is the basis for drawing up the Project Plan and is a separate part of the PID.

Simultaneously with the PID, the stage quality plan is drawn up at the end of the initiation stage as part of the Stage Plan for the first execution stage. The Stage Plan includes the Product Descriptions of all the deliverables in this stage. These Product Descriptions include: the quality requirements the product in question must meet, how these requirements will be tested and by whom. The stage quality plan contains a list of all the checks/tests to be performed in this stage and the people, resources and time required. This ensures that the required people, resources and time will actually be reserved in the final plan and the budget in the Stage Plan.

After the Project Board has approved the Stage Plan and authorised the implementation of the stage in question, the Project Manager authorises the implementation of the various Work Packages for the relevant Team Managers. The Product Descriptions of the deliverables and the checks/tests to be carried out are of course included in the description of a Work Package, but so are the applicable quality processes and procedures, such as the change procedure, the configuration management procedures, the reporting agreements and the escalation procedure.

The Team Manager is responsible for having the relevant checks/tests carried out. The Team Manager must record the results of these checks/tests in the Quality Log. These checks/tests trigger many Project Issues. Authorised changes to earlier approved baselines must be included in the configuration management database. The relevant Product Descriptions must be adjusted correspondingly.

Those who are responsible for project assurance must see to it that the quality processes and procedures are actually followed.

4.6.3 Quality expectations and Acceptance Criteria

What exactly do the products have to comply with? We can make a distinction between the quality expectations and the Acceptance Criteria. Quality expectations are in fact the customer's yardstick for what he expects: not too long, user-friendly, safe, etc. The Acceptance Criteria are concrete and specific values on these yardsticks showing what will satisfy the customer: 'no longer than 1.70 metres', 'instructions in English', 'meets health and safety regulations', etc. These are values for which you can say 'it complies' or 'it does not comply". In quality, of course, you have a tolerance. A well-known subdivision for this is: 'must', 'required', 'nice to have' and 'cosmetic'.

Many users find it difficult to define quality expectations and extremely difficult to specify Acceptance Criteria. This could be because in the past they have not had to think explicitly about such matters. The users therefore often need to be helped by the supplier's experts to arrive at good quality expectations and Acceptance Criteria. There is then a risk that 'for the sake of convenience' users leave the specification of criteria to the supplier's specialists or that none are specified.

To prevent this happening, time and attention must be paid at the start of the project to the quality expectations and Acceptance Criteria. The system of quality reviews for interim products that are delivered in a project makes it possible to adjust the criteria at intervals. Once the first interim products are available, the customer's understanding often improves and the criteria are adjusted. An improvement circle then comes into being that will ultimately lead to the delivery of products the customer can use. Changes should not be seen as an admission of weakness, but if the approach has been good from the start, they are proof that the quality circle is working and are an initial indication that the product to be delivered will meet the customer's final criteria.

The dream garden

Bob and Monica have just moved into a brand new house in a new estate in the suburbs. It's time to lay the garden of their dreams. Friends have given them a good tip: there is a good garden centre nearby. They quickly make an appointment with the garden architect and, while enjoying a cup of coffee in a sun-drenched summer house in the garden centre, Bob makes it very clear: he wants the most attractive and best garden for his money.

To find out just exactly what Bob means, the garden architect asks Bob and Monica both some questions, because it's not just Bob who is the customer.

How big is the garden? Do you both enjoy gardening or does it have to be maintenance-free? Do you both like flowers or do you prefer bushes? Do you want a water feature? Will there be children playing in the garden? Do you want to be able to sit in it or walk about? Have you perhaps seen pictures of your dream garden? Have you perhaps made some sketches? Do you want the garden to be green in the winter?

All these questions are a way of discovering the customers' expectations and of making a list of acceptance criteria. The discussion goes so well that the garden architect agrees to make an offer showing the garden design, the layout and a plan for delivery. He talks about the Project Plan and the Project Quality Plan. All the signs look positive as far as quality is concerned. Bob and Monica go away with a good feeling because the offer contains a number of preventive measures.

The garden architect is a member of the Royal Society of Horticulturists and even holds the ISO 9002 certificate. They also saw that that the garden centre staff attend courses every year to keep up-to-date with developments in the trade. The garden design was absolutely fantastic and even included a 3-D colour print of how the garden would eventually look: exactly as they had imagined.

While the garden was being laid out, the designer and his staff kept precisely to the plan. When it turned out that some of the plant roots were too badly damaged they were replaced immediately (quality control) or Bob and Monica were told when that would be done (quality planning). The offer was a shining example of clarity. Every plant, flower or paving stone was clearly described as regards type, material, size and even the colour of the flowers when in bloom (Product Descriptions). Bob and Monica knew what was being laid or planted, and when this was happening and knew too who to go to with questions or complaints (Project Issues). It was striking that when Monica phoned with a question about the garden, the receptionist could immediately see what had happened and when by looking in the diary (Quality Log).

Another thing they liked was the growth guarantee the gardener gave them for a number of 'difficult' plants. And his promise to come back after the growth season and replace any plants that had not 'taken' at no extra charge (corrective measures).
He did add with a laugh that the new puppy Kelly would have to watch out when digging in the dream garden.

Bob and Monica have got value for money: not only in the form of their beautiful garden, but also in the professional way the garden architect and his staff helped them. The garden architect soon found that he was being kept very busy in the new estate. This was partly due to all the positive tales Bob, now chairman of the residents' association, was telling.

4.7 Configuration Management

All property belonging to organisations must be managed to ensure operational efficiency and effective operations. The totality of property is called the configuration of an organisation. In configuration management terminology the components that make up this property are known as configuration items. Configuration management is the management of the products belonging to the organisation. The standards laid down for such management can be found in the guideline for configuration management, ISO 10007. A project is an organisation within an organisation and for that reason the management of configuration items must be recorded and organised by configuration management. The configuration of the outcome of a project is the total of all the deliverables in that project.

The aim of configuration management in a project is that:
- All products can be easily traced.
- The current status of the various products is always known.
- No unauthorised changes are made to these products.
- Everyone always works with the right products.

Configuration management is not an optional extra. Configuration management must be implemented in every project. The only question is how detailed and how formal configuration management should be. Configuration management is important both for the specialist products and for the management products in a project. Management products are also often changed during the course of a project.

4.7.1 Basic functions
Configuration management consists of 5 basic functions:

1 Planning
Deciding what the required level of configuration management is to be and how that should be reached.

2 Identification
Deciding which components are to be managed.

5 basic functions

3 Management
Protecting and issuing products that are to be changed.
Issuing products according to circulation instructions.

4 Status administration
Current status of the project.
Change history.

5 Verification
Configuration control: is the Configuration database correct?
Is everyone working with the right documents?

Figure 4.13 Basic functions of configuration management

- **Planning** - deciding what the required level of configuration management is to be and how that is to be reached. Matters that have to be arranged during planning are:
  - Deciding which products come under configuration management and which do not.
  - Deciding on the level of detail to be recorded for the various products/ configuration items.
  - Agreeing how configuration management is to be put into practice.

- **Identification** - the current identification and recording of the individual configuration items. The configuration items records are registered in a configuration items database.
- **Management** - the management of the configuration items database, the 'freezing' of the approved products, the distribution of the (possibly changed) products and the information pertaining to this. The management process should be organised by making agreements about how the organisation is to be informed on the status and version of the configuration items. This is also the time to establish who is responsible within the organisation or project organisation for releasing versions and the information pertaining to them. It goes without saying that there is a close link to change control or the deliverables in the project.
- **Status accountability** - besides recording the status, keeping the status records up to date is of crucial importance. Status accountability comprises recording and reporting on the current and historical status of configuration items and the changes that have been implemented.
- **Verification** - guaranteeing that the current status of all configuration items corresponds to the official status of the configuration items as recorded in the configuration items database. It would not be the first or last time that project members on the shop floor have used drawings or other documents that have not yet been approved or that have again been replaced by more recent versions. The Configuration Librarian will regularly have to check that the correct configuration items are being used on the shop floor (audits).

Baseline

A baseline is a coherent total of configuration items that have been approved by the Project Board. A baseline can only be changed with the approval of the Project Board. The status of a baseline is frozen until the status has formally been changed. Lapsed baselines must be retained for the record. This makes it possible to trace the successive historical stages of the configuration items. Status reporting also makes it possible to fall back on an earlier version of the configuration items, should that prove necessary.

Configuration Management Plan

To make it possible for configuration items to be managed, the Configuration Management Plan must be written in the initiation stage. The Configuration Management Plan is part of the Project Quality Plan that is itself part of the PID.

The Configuration Management Plan contains at least:
- An explanation of why configuration management is applied in the project.
- A description of the configuration management method to be used.
- A reference to other relevant configuration management systems.
- Information on how and where the configuration items are stored.
- A description of how the information is stored and how the information can be unlocked.
- The registration method, including that for version management.
- Who is responsible for configuration management.

Often use can be made of existing configuration management procedures being used in the standing organisation. If these are not to be used, it is recommended that the reason for this be indicated in the CMP.

The deliverables in a project are delivered to the customer's organisation. In this organisation these products will form part of the configuration items of this organisation. From efficiency considerations it is therefore important to take account of the way the configuration items are recorded in the new organisation as they are being recorded in the project.

Storing the configuration items not only includes storing physical products, but also the file structure of the digital documents.

It is often a good idea to appoint a separate Configuration Librarian, depending on the size of the project. The Configuration Librarian reports to the Project Manager.

Configuration Item Record

The Configuration Item Records contain all the information that has to be recorded on the configuration items during the project. The very minimum to be included are the project number, the product identification code, the name of the product, the version number, the status and the Product Description. See appendix 7.2.19 for a complete list.

Configuration management and verification

At long last, they were finally moving! Having spent two years in premises far too small for his IT department, Henry was finally able to leave. It seemed such a simple project. Henry only needed to arrange for his IT department to be set up again two streets away. This time he would even have a special computer room with controlled access. The weekend before the move he had made a plan. It clearly described who would do what and when and he and his staff had put stickers on everything. Nothing could go wrong. Shut everything down on Friday, pack up on Saturday, install everything on Sunday, replace the backup, test it on Sunday afternoon and then all go out for a meal. It was certainly pretty hectic and busy but the sticker system had worked and all the old and new PCs, servers, network hubs and the new ADSL lines were connected and working.

Of course everything had taken longer than expected and it was already Sunday evening. Going out for a meal together would have to wait until another time. All Henry needed to do was replace the backup...

That is when things started to go wrong. The tape had apparently put everything back onto the hard discs but it was impossible to log into the network and start up the various programs. Backups had been made all the time (there were never any error messages) but no one had checked that replacing the software would actually work!

4.8 Change Control

By definition, a project operates in a changing environment. Seemingly minor changes can have a major effect on the rest of the project. Change control is a procedure that ensures that changes in a project are implemented in a controlled way.

Changes can involve changes to the specifications of the deliverables or changes in the scope, but can also be changes to the status of the project or a change to the context in which the project is to be carried out.

4.8.1 Why is change control necessary?

Without good change control, changes can often creep into the quality requirements of the deliverables and into the scope of the project. Changes can have a major effect on the technical feasibility, the total cost and the duration time of the project, but also on the benefits the customer wants to achieve with the outcome.

There is a risk that changes result in the plan being altered and that decisions about a further change are made based on the altered plan. Gradually the situation may arise that a project slips away from its original goal (objective drift) and/or scope (scope drift). Another possibility is that budgets are increasingly stretched by small changes. When the balance sheet is drawn up at the end of the project, it then appears that the project has cost far more than was originally estimated and/or has taken far longer.

Implementing changes in an uncontrolled fashion can however also have a negative effect on the acceptance the users and other stakeholders in the project have. Project Managers who implement changes in a project themselves to keep users happy, often get the feeling that they are unable to do anything right. One party might be happy, but another one starts complaining. If the change is cancelled or there is an attempt to compromise, no one is happy!

For that reason it is necessary to employ a strict change procedure in projects and to place the authority to make changes with the highest body in the project: the Project Board. The change procedure must be agreed and recorded before the implementation of the project. The change procedure is recorded in the Project Quality Plan as part of the PID in the initiation stage.

4.8.2 Reasons for changes

Changes can have a great many causes. The needs of the user may change. The customer may impose extra requirements. Organisational changes may occur. Suppliers may contract work out to subcontractors. Suppliers may experience payment problems. Technical and development problems may occur. Developed products may be rejected. Changes can also originate in the project environment, resulting from, for example, a new standard, a move, a change in the people involved in the project, a change in existing processes, new legislation, a new political policy, a new business strategy, etc.

Many changes are caused by increasing insight on the part of the users. The simple fact of the project being initiated makes the user more involved in the issues in question and that can deepen users' insight during the course of the project into what they actually need or want.

Many changes are initiated in the quality review meetings. During the review of completed products the user usually gets a good understanding of what the consequences of his quality system are. This often results in requests to adjust the quality system. These requests have to be treated as separate Requests for Change in the change procedure.

4.8.3 Focus on changes

Changes always relate to the specialist products being produced and to the scope of the project. When analysing the consequences of the change, account must be taken of the effect the change will have on the project as a whole and on the variables like time, cost, quality, scope, health, safety, risks, benefits, etc. Every decision taken about a change must be preceded by an analysis of the consequences of the measures to be taken and how these consequences relate to the consequences of former changes.

4.8.4 Change authority

The Project Board is the highest responsible body within a project that can approve changes or measures for changes. The Project Board may delegate the responsibility for such decision-making to a change authority in projects where the probability is that many changes will take place. Often the Senior User on the Project Board is appointed as change authority for the project.

The Project Board can limit this authority with regard to the impact of the change or with regard to the costs involved. If a major impact is expected and/or higher costs, the change authority has to hand the final decision back to the Project Board. The change authority usually receives its own budget from the Project Board.

4.8.5 Change budget

The Project Board may allocate a separate budget for changes to the scope and/or specifications. Naturally, the Project Board can also set limits on, for example, the budgets for each change or even for each stage. It is particularly advisable to set a change budget for projects in which a great many changes are expected to come from the users and in which the Executive will have no chance to release extra budgets during the course of the project.

4.8.6 Relation to configuration management

Approved changes to the scope or the specifications or rejection of developed products have an effect on configuration management because the products (or configuration items) already in existence need a different status. When changes are made to the specifications, the Product Descriptions must also be adjusted.

5. Techniques

5.1 Introduction

Many techniques can be applied for going through the various processes. Many of these techniques depend upon the type, size and complexity of the project and the professional field and branch within which the project is to be carried out. The application of the various techniques may also vary per country. Other techniques are more universal. Described in this chapter are the following four techniques:

- Product-based planning
- Technique for planning activities and resources
- Technique for quality reviews
- Change control approach

These techniques are considered essential when organising and managing the projects described in this book.

PRINCE2 only recognises the techniques Product-based planning, the Technique for quality reviews and Change control. In addition to these three techniques, this book includes the Technique for planning activities and resources. This technique is viewed as an important aid when going through the Planning process.

5.2 Product-based planning

The latest project management methods are based on product-based planning. A good understanding of the work involved, the time still required and costs involved can only be ascertained by first determining the products to be produced and delivered, what the content of these products is, in what order and the interrelationship between the products.

It also is not possible to make a good estimate of the progress if there are no (provisional) products to act as a support-base for the plan. Estimates of time the time required and costs based on activities still to be carried out are often inaccurate and usually optimistic if there is no clear reference to the different products. The upper management level is also hardly able to or unable to check the estimates based on activities.

Defining (provisional) products also makes it possible to check these products at interim points. In this way, it can be determined in an early stage whether that which is produced meets the customer's quality criteria. In addition, any changes required can be signalled in advance and, if necessary, a change procedure can be started.

5.2.1 Product Breakdown Structure

The first step within the technique product-based planning is to draw up a Product Breakdown Structure. The Product Breakdown Structure gives a hierarchical structure of all the deliverables. These are the end products, the provisional products and the products delivered by third parties in order to make achievement of the final end products possible.

A product breakdown divides the specialist products from the management products. The specialist products are all the products required to deliver the project outcome. The management products are the products required for organising and managing the project. The quality products also fall under the management products. The quality products are the management products which are directly responsible for guaranteeing the quality process (see figure 5.1).

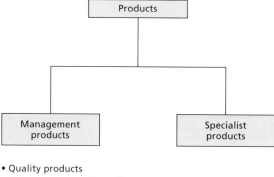

Figure 5.1 Breakdown of products

For each plan it is recommended that a division be first made of the products into specialist products and management products, in order to ensure that the management products are not forgotten. Making management products costs time and money and they must not be overlooked. Usually the specialist products are planned first and the management products are added to the plan at a later date. An overview of the management products is given in figure 5.2. This breakdown is almost always the same for all projects and can be used as a checklist.

In a product breakdown of a plan, the outcome of what the plan must deliver is placed at the top. The outcome is subsequently subdivided into the most important deliverables and these products are again subdivided into the subproducts or components of which they are composed, etc.

The degree to which this is decomposed depends upon the objective of the plan. If the breakdown is part of the Project Plan, then it is not decomposed as much, for example, one of the team plans for the same project. Compare it to the repair of a car. The car owner and the garage will probably discuss the tyres, brakes and engine. The car mechanic and store will discuss the various filters, and the various nuts and bolts. The degree to which the products are decomposed in the plan therefore depends upon who the plan is destined for.

If no separate components of a product need testing by those parties directly involved in the plan, then further subdivision of that product in the breakdown is also of no interest. The further subdivision of that product can then be included under the title 'Composition' in the Product Description of the product concerned.

Figure 5.2 Overview of the management products

Products in the breakdown that are subdivided further are called the provisional products. These provisional products are again separated into composite products and product clusters:
- Composite products must be assessed individually, separate from the assessment of all underlying products.
- Product clusters comprise more underlying products, but the total of these products does not need to be assessed separately.

Product clusters are useful for making a structured decomposition possible. In order to visualise the difference between the composite products and the product clusters, the composite products are given in the Product Breakdown in a rectangle, the same as the singular products and the product clusters are given in a window.

If the software and hardware of a computer has to be tested and later also the complete computer, then it can be indicated in a breakdown with the Computer as a composite product with below the singular products Software and Hardware. An alternative notation is to include all three, the Software, Hardware and the Computer as singular products in the breakdown under the product Workplace. In the first example the Computer is given as a composite product in a rectangle. In the second example the Workplace is given as product group in a rhombus (see fig. 5.3).

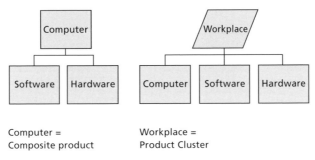

Figure 5.3 Example of a composite product and a product cluster

The breakdown consists of products and therefore of nouns and not activities. In order to be sure that people do not make a mistake, it is preferable to use nouns that cannot at the same time be verbs or to add an adjective to the noun: so preferably not the noun 'Plans', but 'Formulated Plans'.

The same nouns must not repeated in the breakdown, or in the different layers of the breakdown either or in the different product clusters. This leads to irrevocable confusion and mistakes.

The product breakdown must be decomposition: not simply a product divided into just one product. There is then no case of decomposition (see figure 5.4 A). Also a product must not be split up into a time or production sequence. In order to avoid confusion it is therefore advisable not to use arrows in a Product breakdown but lines only. A product in a product breakdown also mustn't be coupled to composite products above it (see figure 5.4 B). If they must be split up one below the other due to lack of space, the singular products must not be connected to each other and only connected to the interim product lying alongside a higher product (see figure 5.5).

The product breakdown is a hierarchical decomposition. This has been chosen purposefully because these subdivisions are diametrically opposite the Product Flow Diagram in the third stage of product-based planning. The Product Flow Diagram is arranged explicitly according to a development sequence. Using two very different subdivisions enables a greater chance of all the deliverables being identified. From the objective of identifying the products it is no longer useful to include more versions or numbers of the same products in the decomposition.

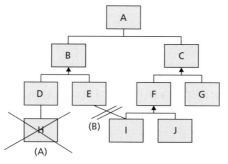

Figure 5.4 Product breakdown

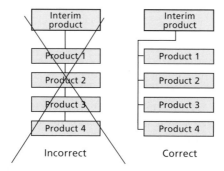

Figure 5.5 Shortened notation

The product breakdown must also include the products that are supplied from external sources or products with which the project is started. It is important that these external products are identified in a project. The input in the projects must also be identified and checked in order to guarantee the quality of the project outcome to be delivered. In this do not indicate where this external product comes from or who has set it up, but indicate the name of the product itself.

A Product Checklist can be compiled based on the product breakdown. This list gives an overview of all the products to be used and to be delivered in a plan. Such a list is particularly useful for large and complex products. In the subprocess, Completing a Plan (PL7), this list is completed with the start and delivery date of the separate products.

5.2.2 Product Descriptions

A Product Description must be drawn up as soon as it is known that such a product must be used or developed within the project. Often little is known of the product itself. That in itself is not so bad. A product name and a product code is sufficient. Most important is that, as soon as a product is identified, a Product Description of the product is included in the quality file. This prevents the setup of a Product Description being forgotten and this resulting in the product not being included in the compilation of the relevant plan and/or the compilation of the test plan.

A Product breakdown must be definitely determined as soon as the plan is compiled in which the product concerned is used or produced. The Product breakdown is frozen with the approval of the plan related to it. In this way a Product Description for product A that must be realised in stage X of the plan is determined and frozen with the completion and approval of the Stage Plan for stage X.

The specified Product Descriptions must be included in the configuration management database. The configuration of the product must not be changed without the formal approval of the same party that also approved the original configuration. For every change in the configuration of the relevant product the Product Description of that product must also be changed accordingly.

The Product Descriptions form the basis for the Work Packages that must be carried out. The Product Descriptions are also useful when requesting tenders. The supplier has a complete overview of all the important information of the product to be produced. The products developed on the basis of Work Packages must also be checked based on the relevant Product Descriptions.

The Product Descriptions include other sources, upon which basis the specific product must be produced. These can be products from which the specific product must be compiled, but these can also be documents who describe how the product is to be produced. Furthermore, the Product Description contains the product composition. For a book this can be the subdivision of the chapters to be written, for a machine it can be the different machine components. The way the product is to be delivered must also be indicated (form and appearance). A document must for example be delivered according to a certain template; A4 and bound. A machine, for example, must be delivered 'packaged, ready for transport by sea'. Finally, included in the Product Descriptions are the measurable quality criteria, the manner in which the product must be checked, and who will carry out the checks.

Quality criteria are given in the Product Description or possibly a referral to specifications which are laid down in another document, such as a programme of requirements. In this case it is recommended to include a version of the relevant programme of requirements and to refer specifically to the relevant chapters of this programme of requirements.

The power of a Product Description is the simplicity and overview. Do not make the Product Descriptions too long: one or two A4's is usually sufficient. In organisations where lots of projects are carried out there are often standard Product Descriptions for specific products available. It is important to involve the people who are going to check the products and/or the people who are going to take the products away when compiling the Product Descriptions.

5.2.3 Product Flow Diagram

Besides the Product Descriptions, it is necessary to know the order in which the products will be used and developed. Therefore the third step in product-based planning is the creation of a Product Flow Diagram. Given in this Product Flow Diagram are all the singular and composite products from the product breakdown in their sequence of development.

The rules for creating a Product Flow Diagram are simple. The flow diagram is drawn from the top down or from left to right. All singular and composite products from the product breakdown are given with exactly the same descriptions as in the product breakdown. All internal products are given in a rectangle. All products started with and products supplied by third parties are given in an ellipse. The sequence in which the products are required is given with arrows. Products can, in principle, only be produced one after the other or in parallel. The flow diagram ends with the project outcome.

In the flow diagram, the specialist products are drawn first, followed by the management products. From the management products only the stage documents and project end documents are given. Periodic management products such as Checkpoint Reports and Highlight Reports, log books, quality products and incident dependent reports such as Exception Reports are not included in the flow diagram. It is wise to include test plans in the flow diagrams because these must first be approved before they are carried out.

When creating a Product Flow Diagram a new product is quite often identified for the plan. These products must be added to the product breakdown in order to be sure that both diagrams are in line with each other. The relevant Product Description must also be written and the Product List updated.

When creating a Product Flow Diagram it is recommended to fill in the flow diagram from the starting point of the plan (from front to back) as well as from the end point of the plan (from back to front). This gives the best results. Furthermore, it is recommended when creating a Product Flow Diagram to involve the people who will carry out the work and who will make use of the outcome.

The sequence of products or parallel relations as given in the Product Flow Diagram, are often only a rough illustration of reality. In a Product Flow Diagram for a Project Plan, products are often given that need further working out in a Stage Plan or Team Plan. Singular products in a decomposition of a Project Plan are often composite products in a Stage Plan or Team Plan. However, it is not recommended to further split the Project Plan or to define more complicated relationships. It is better to accept a simple flow diagram for the Project Plan and to work out the products and the product relations further in the underlying Stage Plans and Team Plans.

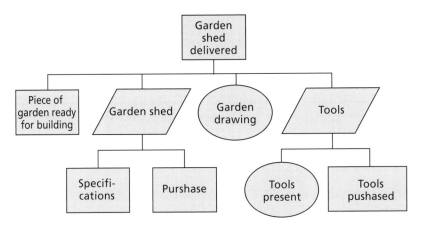

Figuur 5.6 Product breakdown structure 'Garden shed delivery'

Project description 'Purchase'

Project	Garden shed delivery
Product number	01
Name	Garden shed purchased
Objective	Complete garden shed for placement n garden
Composition	Garden shed do-it-yourself kit
	Foundation plates
	Lighting plus wiring
Sources	Garden drawing
	Specifications
Form	Packaged and delivered to home address
Supplier	Garden Centre
Quality criteria	Wood class FSC
	Other requirements in accordance with specifications
Quality review	Inspection certificates and documentation
	Visual inspection of material for amounts and any defects
Assessors	Gardener

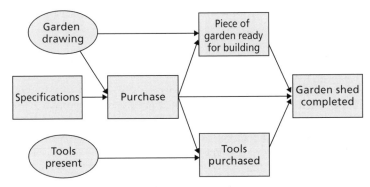

Figure 5.7 Product Flow Diagram 'Garden shed delivery"

5.3 Technique for planning activities and resources

Use is often made of a network planning methodology (PERT or CPM or Precedence) when creating a time schedule in combination with a bar chart (Gantt chart).

The PERT and the CPM methods are based on 'Activity on arrow'. With these methods the activities are given using arrows between the nodes. The Precedence method is a network method based on 'Activity on node'. In this the activities are given in the network nodes. The relationships between the activities are given using arrows between the nodes.

With the Precedence method several types of relationships between the activities can be indicated simply, such as start-start, finish-finish and finish-start relationships. With the Activity on arrow methods this is somewhat more difficult. Furthermore with the Precedence method parallel activities can also be simply illustrated. In an Activity on arrow method a dummy must first be created separately. Finally, the Activity on arrow has the disadvantage that the planning must be calculated in a separate overview. In the Precedence method, the Project Manager can do this in the network plan itself. Practice has shown that the Precedence method is applied more often than other network methods. This book therefore only explains the Precedence method.

5.3.1 Activity on node: Precedence method

Relationships between activities

The various relationships between the activities are given in this method by the way in which the various nodes are connected together. This enables a time delay to be built in. The time delay can be simply indicated by writing the relevant delay next to the connection line between the two activities (see figure 5.8).

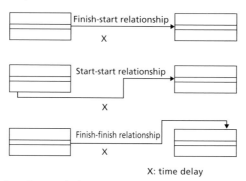

Figure 5.8 Relationships in the Precedence method

Notation at activities nodes

In the Precedence method the nodes that give the activities are drawn in a rectangle as given in Figure 5.9. The information in the rectangle is related to the relevant activity itself and comprises:
- **Early Start (ES)** - earliest possible starting time of the activity in the plan.
- **Late Start (LS)** - latest possible starting time of the activity in the plan.
- **Early Finish (EF)** - earliest possible end time of the activity in the plan.
- **Late Finish (LF)** - latest possible end time of the activity in the plan.
- **Activity** - short description of the activity.
- **Duration (D)** - duration of the activity.
- **Float** - the amount of spare time of the activity in the planning. A distinction is made between the 'total float' and 'free float'.

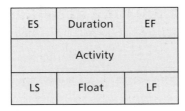

ES	Duration	EF
	Activity	
LS	Float	LF

Figure 5.9 Activity block notation

Precedence method terms

The basis of the method is that first the earliest possible delivery time of the plan is determined. Subsequently the critical path of all the activities and the float of all the separate activities are determined. The earliest possible delivery time is the shortest possible time needed, after starting work, to deliver the plan. The critical path is formed by a series of activities in the plan that directly determines the earliest possible delivery date.

The **total float** of an activity is the time that may be spent carrying out the activity, without the delivery date shifting, assuming that the duration time of all other activities does not change. For all activities on the critical path the total float is zero, in view of the fact that a delay of an activity on the critical path immediately gives the same delay for the delivery date. For all activities that are not on the critical path, the total float per activity may be larger than zero.

In addition to the total float there is the term **free float**. This is the time tolerance that may play a factor in an activity without causing a delay to the following activity, assuming that before this activity the duration time of all other activities remained the same. This float is particularly important for planning the following teams in a project. If the float is not specified, the total float is intended.

Stages plan

The stages in for calculating a plan based on a Precedence method are:
- Identify the activities.
- Identify the mutual relationships between the activities.
- Determine the duration time of the individual activities.
- Draw the network (relationships).
- Calculate through the network from beginning to end and determine the earliest possible delivery date.
- Calculate through the network from end to the beginning.
- Determine the critical path (all activities for which the total float = 0).
- Determine the total float (and the free float) per activity of the other activities.

Identifying the activities and the mutual relationships between the activities is part of the subprocess Identifying Activities and Dependencies (PL3). Determining the duration time of the individual activities is part of the subprocess Estimating (PL4). The other activities are carried out as part of Scheduling (PL5).

Duration times

The duration time of an activity is usually not a hard and fast rule, even when going from a fixed commitment of people and resources. In addition, the time estimated can vary. An optimistic, most probable or most pessimistic value can be assumed. With Planning, the value to be calculated is agreed. Often the choice lies between the most probable and the most pessimistic value. A weighted measured time can also be used based on an average determined from 3 values. A frequently used formula is:

$$D= (1e + 4A +1L)/6$$

$$Duration\ time = (1 \times earliest\ time + 4 \times average\ time + 1 \times latest\ time)/6$$

With the earliest and latest times the assumption is taken that in 90% of the cases duration time of an activity is not exceeded.

When calculating forward in a network plan, a duration time must be chosen per activity. If one wants to work with different duration times then the delivery time must be calculated forward for each combination of duration times in the network planning. Based on the various combinations the most probable delivery time of the complete plan can be calculated.

Precedence method forward and backward pass calculations

When forward-pass calculating in the network, from beginning to end, the Earliest Start (ES) of an activity is determined by adding the duration times of the successive activities leading to that activity. The Earliest Finish (EF) of an activity is determined by adding the Earliest Start (ES) and the Duration time (D) of the relevant activity: EF = ES + D. Where more combinations of activities lead to the start of an activity, the ES is the largest of the EF of the previous activities (see figure 5.10).

Figure 5.10 forward-pass calculating from beginning to end

With backward-pass calculating in the network, from the end to the beginning, the Latest Finish (LS) of the activity is determined by subtracting the duration from the LF of the activity. Where several activity combinations from the end of the activity lead to delivery, the LF is the lowest of the earliest LS moment of successive activities. The LS is determined by LS = LF - D (see figure 5.11).

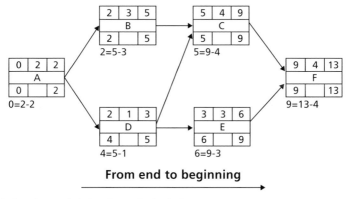

Figure 5.11 Backward-pass calculations from end to beginning

The total float per activity is determined by ES - LS, or by EF - LF. The total float is the time span within which completion of an activity may occur, without the delivery date being pushed back, if all the other activities remain equal.

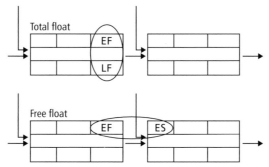

Figure 5.12 Free and total float

The critical path is the combination of activities where the total float of each activity is zero. The other activities lie on the subpaths. Finally, if required the free float per activity can also be determined for the activities. The free float is determined by EF - ES of the first successive activity in the network (see figure 5.12). This free float is shown immediately under the activity block (see figure 5.13).

The free float is the amount of spare time of an activity in relation to any successor activity, if all previous activities are equal.

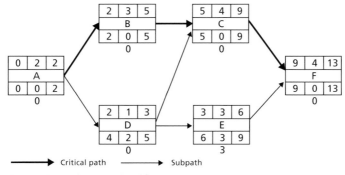

Figure 5.13 Critical path and subpaths, free and total float

5.3.2 Gantt chart

Subsequently, based on the network a Gantt chart can drawn. The Gantt chart provides a graphical illustration of all the activities in a bar chart diagram, where all the activities and their duration times are given on the vertical axis and the horizontal axis gives the total time span. A 'more extensive' version of the Gantt chart gives the most important relationships between the different activities in the planning, the slack in the duration times of activities and the free float of the activities. The slack of an activity is the difference between the duration time which is calculated in the planning and the minimum duration time of the activity. Activities on the critical path can also have slack, but only if there is a task with contingency, otherwise there is no slack on the critical path (see figure 5.12).

A network plan provides an excellent means for analysing a plan. In addition, the various alternatives enable fast forward-pass calculations. That is not possible with a Gantt chart. The advantage of a Gantt chart over a network plan is that the Gantt chart is easier to read and provides a better overview than network plan - essential for team involvement! Furthermore, in a Gantt chart the slack of activities can be illustrated simply in one diagram. The Gantt chart also makes visualisation of the progress of the work easier (in figure 5.14 the position at the end of week 7 is included).

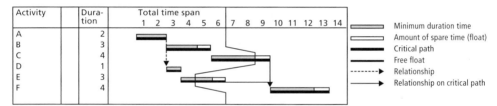

Figure 5.14 Gantt Chart

In a Gantt chart the relationships between the activities do not need to be illustrated. That is often preferred because with too many relationships, readability is reduced and the Gantt chart loses its effect. However, because not all the relationships are illustrated, it is possible that these relationships get forgotten when the plan is changed. This means that the new planning is of no use and the stakeholder parties are often unaware of this. Due to the lack of interrelationships, important basic points are also not noted in a Gantt chart. This can have tremendous consequences if the plan needs to be changed and questions such as 'cause and result' and 'more or less work' should arise. It is therefore strongly recommended to draw a Gantt chart in combination with a network plan and to start by drawing up a network plan.

5.3.3 Planning of people and resources

Based on the network planning and the Gantt chart the commitment of people and resources for the duration of the project can be determined. The Gantt chart is best done manually. A network plan is best done using software. The resource per time unit per activity is determined by dividing the total resource for an activity by the duration time for that activity.

Resource = Total resource/ Duration time

Subsequently, the required resource can be added together per time unit to get the total resource required in that time unit. The overview of all total resources per time unit gives the resource plan for the plan concerned. This resource plan can subsequently be compared with an overview of the availability for the same period (see figure 5.15). If different distinctive types of resources to be controlled are put into a plan, a resource plan must be set up per resource type to be controlled.

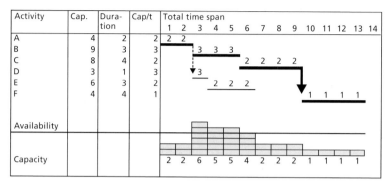

Figure 5.15 Resource planning

Should it become apparent that the required resource is higher than the resource available, in principle a number of different measures are possible. First of all, an attempt can be made to change the resource available to the resource required, possibly by shifting within other projects, so that the required resource can be met. It can also be investigated whether the resource required can be filled by other resource sources: if, for example, there are too few designers but enough draughtsmen, it can be investigated whether the draughtsmen can take on some of the work of the designers.

Activity	Cap.	Dura-tion	Cap/t	Total time span 1	2	3	4	5	6	7	8	9	10	11	12	13	14
A	4	2	2	2	2												
B	9	3	3			3	3	3									
C	8	4	2							2	2	2	2				
D	3	3	1				1	1	1								
E	6	3	2							2	2	2					
F	4	4	1											1	1	1	1
Availability																	
Capacity				2	2	4	4	4	4	4	4	2	1	1	1	1	

Figure 5.16 Optimised resource planning

If none of these options are possible or undesirable, the planning for the activities must be changed. First a check can be made as to whether the activities can be shifted in the plan without putting the delivery date at risk. Another alternative is to lengthen the duration time of these activities so that the demand for resource per time unit is reduced. Sometimes, it can help to split up activities, in order to avoid peak situations. These alternatives are, of course, only possible for activities with float (see figure 5.16). If these activities also do not lead to the desired result, the scope of the plan must be changed or the delivery date for the plan must be moved. Only once agreement has been reached concerning this can finally a definitive time schedule be determined based on the completed resource plan.

5.4 Change control approach

The technique Change control approach gives the procedure for managing changes.

Within PRINCE2 all remarks and comments and (possible) changes within a project are logged as a Project Issue. Project Issues can be:
- **A Change Request** - this is a change to or of one or more products.
- **A Change in Specifications** - one or more products do not meet or will not meet the agreed specifications.
- **General Project Issues** - these are all other changes that may affect the success of the project. This may also include a simple question.

A Project Issue may arise at any time during the project and can be introduced by anyone who is involved or interested in the project. Project Issues must be logged in an Issue Log. A unique number is allocated, plus the author, registration date, type and the priority of Project Issue.

5.4.1 A possible change procedure
- Log Project Issues in the Issue Log. Determine the first priority. React to misunderstandings. Return a copy of the registration to the author (CS3).
- Analyse the consequences (impact analysis) in time, costs, quality, scope, benefits and risks and if necessary update the Risk Log. Determine the priority of the Issue in consultation with the Senior User. Determine the possible measures to be taken (CS4).
- Review the possible measures versus the consequences (costs/benefits analysis) within the status perspective in which the stage or the project is in and determine the measures to be taken (CS5).
- If a Request for Change is concerned, create a Request for Change and put it to the Project Board for approval (CS7).
- The Project Board will subsequently make a decision concerning the Request for Change (SP4).
- After approval by the Project Board, take corrective measures, update the Issue Log and report back to the author. The Configuration Librarian updates the configuration management database (CS7).
- Assignment of the relevant work (CS1).

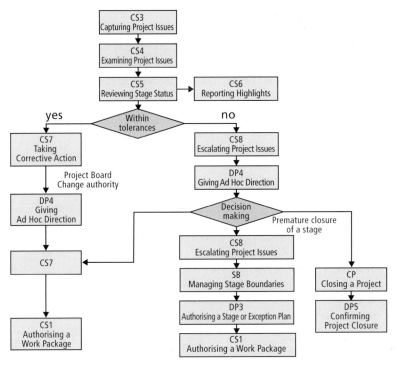

Figure 5.17 A possible change procedure

As a result of the Project Issue, there is a danger of the Stage Plan exceeding the given tolerances; the Project Manager must then follow the agreed escalation procedure. The Project Manager must produce an Exception Report and submit it to the Project Board (CS8). The Project Board can subsequently decide whether one of the options presented in the Exception Report needs to be worked out further (DP4). The Project Manager is given the assignment to work out this option in an Exception Plan. The Project Manager will trigger the stage Managing Stage Boundaries (CS8). From this process the Project Manager will create an Exception Plan together with the End Stage Report (SB), and submit this is to the Project Board (DP3) for approval in a separate meeting (Exception assessment).

However, the Project Board can also decide to proceed normally with the project, despite the threat of the given tolerances being exceeded. The Project Board normally takes additional measures outside the project in order to guarantee the progress and Business Case of the project. The Project Board instructs the Project Manager of which additional measures are to be taken concerning this (DP4). The Project Manager sees to it that the agreed measures are carried out, updates the Issue Log and reports back to the author reporting the Project Issue. The Configuration Librarian updates the configuration management database (CS7).

Finally, the Project Board may decide that there is no point in continuing with the project and instructs the Project Manager to prematurely end the project (DP4). The Project Manager will start the process Closing a Project (CP), draw up and submit the necessary documents for approval to the Project Board to disband the project (DP5).

5.4.2 Priority

A priority can be allocated to each Project Issue. Allocating a priority is a good way of providing insight into the importance of the change in relation to the project. Implementing many unnecessary changes can be avoided this way. A possible way of prioritising is:

- **Highest priority (must)** - if the change is not implemented the project will not achieve the desired outcome.
- **High priority (required)** - if the change is not implemented it will have serious consequences for the desired outcome. However, with a temporary change in procedure, for example, it may be possible to work with it.
- **Normal priority (nice to have)** - it is preferable to carry out the change but it is not crucial for the outcome.
- **Low priority (cosmetic)** - a cosmetic change, for example.

5.4.3 Impact analysis

The Project Manager must investigate the impact of all (proposed) changes in order to assess the consequences of the changes. The intended benefit of possible changes must be weighed against any possible additional costs and the increased risk of a longer duration time. It is the Project Manager's task to give a good overview of all the options, including the advantages and disadvantages, so that the Project Board can make a well-founded decision.

Often a problem within projects is the continual implementation of yet more new changes. Despite the change being properly approved, it is up to the Project Manager to keep a continuous watch on the scope (what must the project deliver) of the project. Changes can otherwise degenerate into project 'scopedrift', where slowly but surely the original objective of the project Business Case is lost. Implementing changes often takes a lot of energy, time and money and takes the attention away from what must actually be achieved. The creation of a change authority and allotting priorities usually helps limit the number of Request for Changes being implemented.

It is also possible that successive changes contradict each other. A kind of yo-yo effect then takes place. This often occurs because the consequences of the changes have not been sufficiently investigated. This yo-yo effect also often occurs if the Project Manager makes independent decisions on a Request for Change. His position often does not give him enough authority to turn away a Request for Change. After all, these requests come from the customer users. By creating a change authority from the customer organisation this effect can be contained.

5.4.4 An Off-Specification

An Off-Specification usually goes through different procedures to the Request for Change. If the consequences of the Off-Specification fall within the agreed stage tolerances, then the responsible party is usually given the first opportunity to repair the Off-Specification. Should this not work, then the Request for Change route is followed. Moreover, sometimes the Project Board accepts an Off-Specification without demanding any further corrective measures. This is called a concession.

Should an Off-Specification lead to the stage tolerances being exceeded, then the Project Manager must create an Exception Report and the escalation procedures must be followed.

5.5 Quality review technique

A quality review is a structured and organised approach to assessing the quality of a product particularly for the predefined quality criteria. Is the product complete? Does it have the right relationship with other products? Does the preliminary product lead to an outcome that will meet the requirements set? Documents in particular can be assessed in this manner for content and cohesion.

The product is first sent to all the stakeholder parties to be assessed, together with the Product Description compiled and agreed earlier. These parties assess the product and return the product with comments. The author adds in any small and accepted corrections. Subsequently, other comments are discussed in the meeting with all stakeholders and the author of the product. Based on this, the meeting decides whether the product meets the requirements, or whether corrective measures are necessary. Question points are also identified and additional requirements or wishes are defined. The corrective measures are subsequently implemented by the author. The question points and the additional requirements or wishes are passed on to the Project Manager as Project Issues for action. The product can be endorsed as soon as the corrective measures have been carried out.

5.5.1 Advantages of a quality review
The advantages of a quality review are:
- **Objective of quality assessment** - the product is assessed in a structured and objective manner against the predefined quality criteria.
- **Early identification of defects in products** - any defects are identified at an early stage mainly to achieve a definite development and delivery of the end products.
- **Creation of a platform for quality improvements** - users often only realise what they have requested and what they really want when they see the outcome for the first time of the predefined quality requirements. They may differ a great deal. We call this 'advance insight'. This is annoying because it leads to changes. If this is not determined and picked up in an early stage, it can lead to permanent tensions and negative consequences in a later stage of the project.
- **Creation of a support-base** - the fact that all stakeholders are directly or indirectly involved in the assessment creates a support-base for decision making and for the subsequent acceptance of the product outcome based on the preliminary product.
- **Provision for decision making** - individuals often daren't approve or disapprove products on the grounds of quality. The presence of a predefined Product Description and coming to agreements in a meeting means that decisions are made. Each person only needs to take responsibility for his or her aspect of the assessment.
- **It provides for objective progress checks** - it is often difficult to objectively asses the progress of the work at an early stage. A quality review simply determines whether the product is ready.

5.5.2 Context
In the Planning (PL) process the Product Descriptions of the products to be developed are compiled. This includes a description of the quality specifications for the products, how the quality check will be carried out (by a quality review or not) and who will perform the check.

For the products to be developed in a stage, the relevant Product Descriptions will be defined when preparing the Stage Plan (SB1). The quality review is also planned and the time required, expertise and target date defined.

The Project Manager directs the work to the Team Manager by authorising the relevant Work Package (CS1). The Team Manager accepts the Work Package (MP1). With the transfer, the Project Manager will ensure that the quality reviews are planned in the Team Plan.

The actual quality reviews are performed as part of the subprocess Executing a Work Package (MP2). The quality review results will be registered in the Quality Log by the Team Manager. The Project Manager makes use of these Quality Log entries when assessing the progress of a stage (CS2).

5.5.3 Quality review stages

The quality review comprises the following 3 steps:
1. Preparation.
2. Quality review meeting.
3. Subsequent actions.

Preparation

The quality review is planned during the preparation of a Stage Plan, including who will take part. Subsequently, the relevant Work Package is passed on to the Team Manager who is responsible for its execution. The Team Manager works out the details of the quality review, names the chairman in consultation with the Project Manager and records the agreements about the review with all the individual people.

As soon as preparation for the quality review needs to start, the chairman investigates whether the product to be assessed is actually ready. The chairman investigates whether all reviewers are also available on the review date and whether they have enough time to assess the product in advance. The chairman must select other reviewers in consultation with the Team Manager and Project Manager if this is not already the case. Finally, the chairman confirms the date for delivering comments and the meeting date of all stakeholder parties.

The producer sends the product to all reviewers for assessment, together with the Product Description and a blank question list. Each reviewer assesses the product based on the Product Description and notes down possible defects and questions on the question list. Small defects, such as spelling mistakes can be corrected immediately, and are simply annotated on the product copy. The question list and the product with small corrections are returned by the reviewers to the producer. The small and clearly visible defects are processed by the producer and explanations are given where necessary. Based on the remaining question points, the producer together with the chairman prepares for the meeting and sets out a meeting agenda.

Quality review meeting

The main point of the review is to explain, discuss and come to an agreement about the remaining question points or the individual reviews. It is therefore recommended that, where possible, the reviewer questions and similar question points of the various reviewers are combined as one agenda discussion point. The producer first gives a brief explanation, the question point is discussed and finally 'how to go further' is investigated per question point. It must be determined whether the product meets the various parts of the specification. If this is not the case, then direction towards a solution must be given.

When discussing the question points it is important to make a division between whether the product meets the quality requirements laid down in the Product Description and whether in retrospect the reviewers had something else in mind. In the last case, the product does meet the requirements, but with the review gives one or more parties reason to submit a change proposal. A Change Proposal must NOT be agreed in the review but always reported as a Project Issue to the Project Manager for the Project Manager to pursue further.

The different parties in the meeting will sometimes not agree on whether the product meets the quality requirements. Many quality requirements can be interpreted differently. This discussion point must be reported as a Project Issue to the Project Manager for the Project Manager to pursue further.

The outcome of the quality review can mean that the product is immediately approved. The product can then be signed off in the meeting by the parties present. Another possible outcome is that a few corrections are needed, but that the product can be approved following this. Finally, the conclusion may be that new assessment is necessary after corrections have taken place. These take place separately from the Project Issues that have already been introduced.

Subsequent actions
The chairman reports the outcome of the review to the Team Manager responsible. The producer draws up a plan in consultation with the Team Manager for the corrective work and carries this out. After the repair work has been carried out the corrections are assessed and signed off. It is possible for this to take place via a shortened procedure by including only a few parties in the review. The Project Manager takes care of any Project Issues raised.

5.5.4 Roles in a quality review
Within the quality review, the following roles can be distinguished:
• The producer
• The reviewers
• The chairman
• The Project Manager
• The Team Manager
• The Scribe

The producer
The producer is the person who has created the product or has led the team responsible. The producer distributes the product to the reviewers. The producer is also responsible for carrying out corrective work.

The reviewers
The reviewers are the people who assess the product based on the quality criteria given in the Product Description. The reviewer puts together the question list and indicates the defects in preparation for the quality review. The reviewer takes part in the actual review meeting. He signs the outcome off for agreement.

The chairman
The chairman prepares for the review meeting and is responsible for correct procedures during the review meeting. The chairman also puts together the agenda for the meeting. It is important to assess the product in the meeting and not the producer. The chairman informs the Team Manager about the outcome of the meeting. The chairman finally signs the product off for definite approval and draws up the 'agreed actions' report.

The Project Manager
The Project Manager includes the quality review in the Stage Plan and records this in the Work Package. The Project Manager monitors whether the quality review actually takes place as agreed. Furthermore, he ensures that Project Issues ensuing from the review are followed up. The Project Manager can also act as a reviewer.

The Team Manager
The Team Manager plans the quality review in detail and ensures that the quality review takes place according to plan. The Team Manager records the outcome of the review in the Quality Log and reports the progress to the Project Manager in the Checkpoint Report.

The Scribe
The Scribe assists the chairman by recording and distributing the agreed action points (including the responsibilities).

5.5.5 Project Assurance
The people responsible for Project Assurance can appoint reviewers. They must ensure that the reviewers are fully aware of what is expected of them. Furthermore, they must also ensure that the quality review procedure is followed correctly and that subsequent actions are adequately managed. If necessary, they can also act as reviewers in the quality review.

5.5.6 Success criteria
A quality review is an important instrument for the Project Manager in managing a project. However, if a quality review is not performed correctly, participants can become frustrated and it becomes counter productive. Plenty of attention must be paid to the quality review, particularly when it is performed for the first time.

It is important that:
- The review is directed at indicating defects and not at correcting them. Do not solve problems in the review. That will sooner or later lead to endless discussions and spoils the atmosphere in the meeting. Allow reviewers to limit themselves to determining a direction for the solution. The underlying principle of a successful quality review is the identification of faults and not finding solutions for them.
- Select reviewers on the intrinsic contribution they have to offer and not on the basis of their position.
- Select reviewers such that all concerns in the project are represented. In other words, not simply the immediate users, but also other stakeholders involved in with the project. Also ensure that other relevant teams within the project are represented.
- Appoint an independent chairman. The Project Manager or Team Manager is not 'considered' for the chair position. If they also have a role as reviewer it is not wise to combine this with that of the chair position.
- The product description must be drawn up before start of the stage and approved. Otherwise there is no objective reference point and there is an increased chance that the review turns into a game of 'is-is not'.
- Make sure the review is well-prepared. Start on time. All participants must have received the relevant documents and have studied the product before the review takes place. Ensure that essential people are not absent from the review.
- Only hold the review for the 'important' products. Avoid overkill.

6. Project environment

6.1 Various terms

For clear communication it is important to agree on the meaning of the various terms that we come up against in the practice of project management. In this chapter a number of these terms are explained:

- The difference between projects and programmes
- Multi-project
- Project portfolio
- Large project

6.1.1 Project versus Programme

Included in the first chapter of this book is the following definition of a project:

> *A project is a temporary organisation created for the purpose of delivering one or more business products according to a specified Business Case.*

The Executive is ultimately responsible for exploiting the outcome and achieving the projected benefits. The benefits are only realised once the project has been closed. A programme on the other hand is more than simply delivering an outcome. With a programme there is also the responsibility of achieving the benefits or part of the benefits during the course of the programme. A programme is defined as:

> *A programme is all the projects and activities included in a temporary organisation for achieving one or more of the predefined strategic corporate objectives.*

A programme achieves one or more corporate objectives of strategic importance. A programme is a temporary management structure covering all projects and a temporary management structure in between the projects and the (top) management of the corporate organisation in order to ensure that new corporate objectives involving change are achieved in a structured manner.

In general the outcomes of several joint projects are needed in order to achieve specific corporate objectives. The duration time of a programme is longer than the duration time of related projects.

A programme must consciously be stopped. With a programme, the pros and cons concerning the investments in the change and the benefits to be achieved to justify the existence of a separate (programme) organisation must be weighed up. In practice, a time will come when it is no longer necessary to manage the changes in a separate organisation from a programme, but that this can better be done in the line organisation. The programme can then be disbanded and the programme organisation discharged by the Programme Director. The end of a programme must therefore be self determining and is not a direct consequence of a predefined outcome as with a project, where delivery of the outcome automatically signals the end of the project.

The benefits are defined from the corporate objectives of an organisation that must be achieved with the programme. Therefore, a programme must develop a number of activities besides carrying out a number of projects in order to exploit the outcomes. The organisation must be prepared for the changes to be implemented. The outcomes of projects must be implemented in the organisation, the organisation must work with the new possibilities and it must be ensured that the new method of working is 'business as usual' and that the corporate objectives are actually achieved with these new possibilities.

6.1.2 Multi-project management

Multi-project management is the management of a group of projects that are not interrelated other than optimum use being made of the same people and resources within these projects.

Projects start from a customer-supplier environment. The supplier develops the actual outcomes of the project and provides the people and resources for this. Multi-project management is the responsibility of the supplier's corporate management organisation.

Within multi-project management the control and commitment of people and resources is optimized in these - intrinsically separate - projects. The following matters are important in this:
- The development of a common reporting structure and of shared methods and techniques can lead to better harmony between the projects and corporate organisation.
- Combining project related activities within a corporate unit can enable other units to continue concentrating on their primary responsibilities.
- Shared purchasing of products and services and/or shared contracting in of staff can lead to 'economy of scales', but also to further professionalism of purchasing and contracting.
- Setting up a common corporate office can lead to better support for projects, both quantitatively and qualitatively.
- Commitment of people and resources can be improved by making use of 'pools'.

In addition, in a supplier organisation the projects have a relationship that rises above using the same people and resources. Often various projects are carried out using the same Executive and in this way a dependence exists. Also, they can be directed from a certain market or from a certain competency that one wishes to develop further. This can also be managed within multi-project management.

6.1.3 Management of portfolio projects

Portfolio management covers the management of a group of projects that together supply new possibilities ('capabilities') that are necessary in order to achieve one or more mutual corporate objectives.

Projects start from a customer-supplier environment. The customer is the person or group that has ordered a project and who will profit from the outcome. Portfolio management is the responsibility of the customer's corporate management organisation.
Projects are prioritised and projects controlled by mutual arrangement from the corporate objectives to be achieved on the one hand, and the improvements that need to be implemented for this and the available commitment of people and resources on the other hand. The various projects sometimes deliver a 'solitary' outcome and sometimes in clusters of a number of outcomes that can each provide the organisation with added value. With all the added values the organisation is able to achieve its corporate objectives.

The added value is not achieved within portfolio management, but in ensuring delivery of the various projects and in their interrelationships. Portfolio management is therefore not the same as programme management but a part of programme management.

6.1.4 Large projects

Essentially there is no difference between a 'small' project and a 'large' project. A product or service still needs to be delivered. A large project, however, is a project that comprises a number of part projects, each of which is controlled as an individual project, with its own Executive, its own Project Board and its own Project Manager. Above the various Project Boards is a Project Board that is ultimately responsible for the complete project. The construction of a space shuttle is a large project as is the construction of the channel tunnel. However, the outcome, what is delivered, is still a product. It is up to the customer to use the product and to achieve the objectives with it. Therefore, it is a project and remains a project, and not a programme.

The difference between a portfolio of projects and a large project is that within a portfolio of projects the various projects sometimes deliver a solitary outcome and sometimes clusters of a number of outcomes that can each provide the organisation with added value, whilst with a large project one inseparable combined total outcome is delivered.

A large project, of course, makes use of the same methods and techniques as multi-project management and the management of a portfolio of projects, and these techniques can also be found in the management of programmes

6.2 Programme management

Programme management provides a framework for defining and implementing changes in an organisation. This framework covers making a view explicit (see paragraph 6.2.2), defining the blueprint (see paragraph 6.2.3) and providing the added value of the future situation for the organisation, as well as the organisation and processes in order to implement changes and achieve the added value.

Within programme management the necessary projects are identified and started, the interrelationship of the projects is coordinated and the project outcomes to be delivered are tailored to one another. In addition, programme management covers identifying the added value of changes for the corporate organisation. The added values are made explicit and managed throughout the life of the programme.

The basis for the programme must lie in the contribution of the objectives to be achieved in the programme to the corporate strategy in relation to work to take place. The basis for a programme is laid down in the Business Case. The Business Case must be checked throughout the life span of the programme.

6.2.1 Programme management environment

Corporate strategies can be implemented by individual company sections. Usually several company sections are involved in achieving the corporate strategy. It is recommended therefore to define programmes in order to achieve corporate strategies. Programmes make it possible to implement strategies over several company sections.

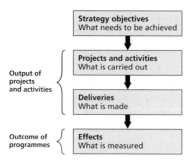

Figure 6.1 Output of projects and outcome of programmes

Essential to a successful programme is that dominant corporate strategies are established in the corporate organisation and that they are supported by management and those carrying out the work. Furthermore, it is important that programmes are able to anticipate change in the corporate strategy and can be changed to the new initiatives.

Programmes trigger projects where new products and/or services are developed that are needed to implement corporate strategies, until the future vision becomes reality and the added value of the programme is achieved.

A clear picture of the future corporate organisation needed to develop the new corporate vision is essential for the establishment of programmes. This picture, the blueprint of the new organisation, must be clear and unambiguous to all parties and remain so for the duration time of the programme.

Figure 6.2 shows the dependencies between projects and programmes.

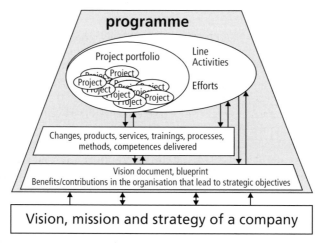

Figure 6.2 Dependencies between projects and programmes

6.2.2 Vision document
A vision document is a description of:
• The products and services that the organisation wants to deliver.
• The markets and customers that the organisation wishes to serve.
• The market position that the organisation wishes to take.

- The level of service that the organisation wishes to offer.
- The relationship the corporate organisation wishes to have with the environment in general and with its customers, competitors, suppliers and employees in particular.

6.2.3 Blueprint

A blueprint is a description of the new corporate organisation with which the situation, as given in the vision description, can be realised including the transitions in between. The blueprint includes a description of the people, work processes, structures, quality systems, information and reporting systems as well as the necessary infrastructure.

6.3 Projects in programmes

As indicated earlier a programme has only one or a number of projects including several activities. Think, for example, of setting and starting up a warehouse as a programme, where all sorts of projects are necessary in order to develop it. The objective of the programme is then formulated in terms of profit figures, stocks, number of customers (per time unit), etc. Projects can therefore be: setting up a shop, laying car parking spots, contracting in personnel, etc. Yet, activities are needed, such as purchasing and selling of products, to develop this and to achieve the benefits.

Depending upon the organisation structure, the Project Boards of the various projects are acquired with the programme organisation. Usually the role of Executive will be filled by the programme manager or a person directly delegated to do so. In most cases a coordinating Project Support and Project Assurance will be set up. This provides great support to the communication in the programme and across the projects. In this way the underlying projects will get much of the required information from the programme. And vice versa, for attention points beyond projects, the information flows more easily to others involved in the programme.

When starting a project within a programme there is usually a good overview of the main points of what has to take place. The Project Mandate will contain a large part of the information required to make a Project Brief. Even if it concerns planning, a project will have to aim at the expectations of the programme. However, this must not be taken literally just like that. It is still important to continually assess how realistic this information is. That is the responsibility of project management. During the programme project tolerances will be defined that are recorded in the Project Brief and in the PID.

The Project Brief is supplied by the programme. The Business Case and the project outcomes are linked to the benefits that must be achieved by the programme. The project is controlled upon the basis of the deliveries related to the benefits upon which the programme is calculated.

Each change that influences areas outside the project must be tailored to programme management strategy and where necessary programme management must make the decisions. An example here can be the change of objectives or of predefined project outcomes, as well as changes to the Business Case.

6.4 Managing change

Often projects and programmes are used by organisations to structure change processes. And, today changes in organisations are the norm. However, change often causes unrest in an organisation. In order to greatly improve the chance of success of change, use can be made of methods and techniques to structure the change process. In the book "Ondernemen binnen de onderneming", Weggeman states six different elements that are important for change in an organisation[4]:
- Strategy
- Personnel
- Management
- Systems
- Structure
- Culture

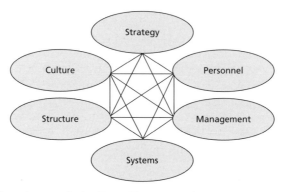

Figure 6.3 Elements for change in an organisation (Source: Weggeman 1985)

These six elements are important for each change in a company and cannot be seen as separate units. Changes in one element have consequences for all the other elements.

A change process arranged according to these elements can act as a support in the process. The consequences per element can be investigated for the organisation. This again gives insight into the change and increases the change of success.

Moreover, in 1995 Prof. J.P. Kotter (Harvard University) defined eight stages for changes in organisations, namely[5]:
- Determine the need for change.
- Formation of a strong sponsor group.
- Formulate a vision.
- Communicate the vision.
- 'Empowering' management with the implementation of changes.
- Realisation of 'quick wins'.
- Establishing the improvements and achieving additional improvements.
- Institutionalisation of the new method of working.

---

4 Weggeman, Mathieu et al. *Ondernemen binnen de onderneming*. Kluwer, 2000.
5 Kotter, John P. *Leading Change*. Harvard Business School Press, 1995.

That many of these methods have been developed out of practice is clear from Gert Wijnen's vision on change. A great analogy can be seen between the change process he has written about and Kotter's eight stages. Wijnen characterises the change process as five steps to be gone through in succession[6]:
1. Raising awareness.
2. Determining the position and developing the vision.
3. Constructing a support-base.
4. Achieving change.
5. Establishment.

The five stages are gone through during each stage of the change.

Each change will cause 'pain' in an organisation. This may occur at any place and at any level of an organisation. The pain is caused by a difference between the desired and the current situation. This brings about awareness for the need to change to the desired situation. Stage 1 in the change process is the awareness of this need right up to the level responsible in the organisation.

The next stage, determining the position and developing the vision, must provide depth to the need from stage 1. A change for the sake of change only leads to trouble. Change driven by a clear and well-defined vision can generate energy. For this the vision and strategy of the change must be well established in the organisation. Furthermore, the need for the change must be made explicit. This process frequently generates a number of concrete plans for improvement and scores points in the short term.

As third stage, the change must be made known throughout the organisation, primarily to create a support-base and involvement. This stage is also the period in which it is useful to score points in the short term by achieving initial outcomes. This will aid in creating a broader support-base in the organisation. A support-base can be achieved by allowing the involvement of the employees concerned in the change process. That is possible in several ways, including joint thought processes and assisting in decision making.

In the stage realisation of the change, there is a support-base in the organisation and it is clear what needs to take place. Now is the time to implement definitive changes. The structuring and form of this will in general take place through projects. Here too use is made of an improvement cycle. Consider here the Deming-circle (Plan-Do-Check-Act).

Establishment is the last stage in the change process. Here it concerns the actual application of the new situation in day to day practices. Here the benefits must be generated that gave the reason for change. The return from the change directly depends on the support in the organisation for the new situation. If employees do not see the advantage of, for example, working in a new way, then it will have a negative influence. It is therefore necessary to involve the employees, or users in PRINCE-2 terms, as early as possible, to promote acceptance.

Each stage in the change process brings the organisation closer to the change. It must be investigated per situation how this step can best be taken. It is important to be aware of the fact that each method acts as a guide and is not a guarantee to success. Each situation demands an individual and involved interpretation.

---

6 Wijnen, Gert et al. *Projectmatig Werken*. Het Spectrum, 2004.

6.5 Different project types

Managing projects is in essence the same regardless of the sector in which the project is implemented. In practice, however, it seems that there is a different interpretation per sector. The interpretation of project management in construction differs from the interpretation in the IT-sector or with culture projects. The setup and control of large and small projects also differs from that of mono-disciplinary and multi-disciplinary projects. However, in all cases the basic process diagram is the same. Per project and per environment the basic diagram can, however, be made to measure.

The following list gives a number of project types that frequently take place in practice:
• Mono-disciplinary and multi-disciplinary projects.
• National and international projects.
• Large and small projects.
• Commercial projects and (semi-)government projects.
• Projects in large and small organisations.
• Projects within the various branches such as logistics, provision of services, etc.
• R&D projects, infrastructural projects, IT-projects.
• Organisation change projects and cultural projects.

If a look is taken at the different project types, the question rises as to whether to classify these projects and whether useful things can be said per classification about how projects must be approached within this classification. That does appear to be possible. There are 2 variables recognisable in each project type or sort. On the one hand one has projects where the 'goal' or 'product' is clearly, or not clearly defined; the so-called 'product assurance' of the project. On the other hand there are projects where the 'method of working' or 'processes' are clear, or unclear. In order to make a division between the various types of projects, Turner & Cochrane have made a subdivision based on methods and clearly defined goals[7].

The principle behind this arrangement is that the better defined the methods and objectives are, the better chance of success the project has. The opposite also applies, the less defined the methods and objectives are, the less chance of success it has without 'good' project management.

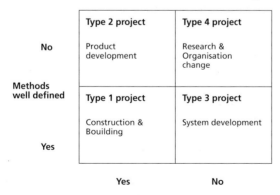

Figure 6.4 Matrix of objectives and methods (Source: Turner & Cochrane)

---

7 Turner J.R., and Cochrane R.A. *Goals and Methods Matrix: Coping with Projects with Ill Defined Goals and/or Methods of Achieving Them.* International Journal of Project Management, May 1993, Vol 11, No 2.

6.5.1 Type 1 projects (objectives and methods well defined)

Projects of type 1, in particular, are operational projects and are also called classic projects. They are projects with well-known aspects that are structured and executed according to an established plan. That is why linear staging applies: first analyse, then design, subsequently achievement and finally delivery. This is also called the 'waterfall method'.

The compulsory stages are still needed in order to set decision times with the sponsor or business manager. In general, the projects are product-based and the project employees are specialists in this field due to the repetition of the work. This means that there are fewer uncertainties and because the work has been done frequently, there is a wealth of experience acting as a base for a planning which can be worked out in detail in advance. In addition, any possibility of risks and their consequences can be estimated and account taken of them in the plans. Due to lots of routine work the Project Manager can concentrate on other methods of efficient practice. Thee projects have an increased chance of success.

A fitting style of project management is controlling as an **administrator/manager**.

6.5.2 Type 2 projects (objectives well defined, methods not)

In this project type the objective is well defined but how that objective is to be achieved is not (yet) clear. Here product development projects can be thought of that are often multi-disciplinary. Often the duration time is a priority because 'time to market' determines the Business Case and this puts the project under pressure. Because there are many uncertainties concerning the method of approach, these projects usually first have a pre-research stage (feasibility study) in which the method of approach leading to the best outcome is determined. This means that the project is function-based from the start and changes to system-based or product-based as soon as a large proportion of uncertainties have been removed from the project. The detailed planning is made per stage and a review takes place per stage. A notable point here is that user involvement is greatest at the start and the end of the project. During the project this is almost zero.

A fitting style of project management is that of (team) **supervisor**.

6.5.3 Type 3 projects (method well defined, objectives not)

These are projects where the specific requirements and wishes of the user are not or not specifically defined. These must evolve during the course of the project. In these project types the challenge lies primarily with the first project stages. A regular interchange must take place between analysis and the design of the appropriate approach. This approach is also called the 'development stage' or the 'spiral model'. It can help to use prototypes where the users are quickly confronted with tangible outcomes and based on this continue further or design a new product. In this way the requirements evolve during the project.

The projects are tactical or operational by nature and at the start function based. As the outcomes become more specifically defined this changes into module or component based. With this type of project the involvement of the user is also limited to the start and end. The execution stage is chiefly in the hands of specialists.

A fitting style of project management is therefore also **advisory**.

6.5.4 Type 4 projects (methods and objectives not well defined)

Characteristic for this type of projects is that there are many uncertainties: experience is lacking concerning the work to be done and the consequences of the risk can be serious. These projects are difficult to plan and are therefore worked out and planned in detail stage by stage. The complexity is often extremely high because sometimes vague ideas must deliver specific results. In view of the tremendous impact for the user involvement throughout the complete project is necessary. This is particular recognisable in Research & Development projects. Project Manager and users must effectively follow the same route to achieve the required outcome. We call this the 'evolutionary project method'. One takes a part of the product, develops it completely, learns from it and implements this in the following realisation stage. By taking small well-organised steps (stages) the users gain insight into the final product and experience the method of working.

A fitting style of project management would be an adventurous **explorer** sometimes taking two steps forward and one back.

6.5.5 PRINCE2 application

Obviously, in reality a project comprises not just one of these four types but a mixture of all sorts of forms. This means that the Project Manager together with the Executive for each project must again investigate the specific characteristics of the project and that the Project Manager must then aim in this direction. PRINCE2 is a generic method for project management, such that the methodology can be used as a basis for designing and managing all types of projects.

7. Appendices

7.1 Glossary of terms

Term	Description
Acceptance Criteria	A prioritised list of criteria that the final product(s) must meet before the customer will accept them; a measurable definition of what must be done for the final product to be acceptable to the customer. They should be defined as part of the Project Brief and agreed between customer and supplier no later than the project initiation stage. They should be documented in the project Initiation Document.
Activity network	A flow diagram showing the activities of a plan and their interdependencies. The flow diagram shows each activity's duration, earliest start and finish times, latest start and finish times and float. See also 'Critical Path'.
Baseline	A snapshot of a position or a situation. Although the position may be updated later, the authorised document does not change. It remains available as a record of the original state and as such can be compared with the current position.
Benefits	The positive outcomes, quantified or unquantified, that a project is being undertaken to deliver, and that justify the investment.
Business Case	Information that describes the justification for setting up and continuing a PRINCE2 project. The Business Case provides the reasons for the project. It is updated at key points throughout the project.
Change authority	One or more people to whom the Project Board may delegate responsibility for consideration of the requests for change. The change authority is given a budget and can approve changes within that budget.
Change budget	The money allocated to the change authority to be spent on authorised requests for change.
Change control	The procedure to ensure that the processing of all Project Issues is controlled, including the submission, analysis and decision-making.
Checkpoint	A team-level, time-driven review of progress, usually involving a meeting.
Checkpoint Report	A Checkpoint Report of the information gathered at a checkpoint meeting, which is given by a team to the Project Manager and provides reporting data as defined in the PID.
Communication Plan	Part of the Project Initiation Document describing how the project's stakeholders and interested parties will be kept informed during the project.
Concession	An Off-Specification that is accepted by the Project Board without corrective action.

Configuration audit	An evaluation of the latest status of the Configuration Management Database with the information held by the product authors or the individual products.
Configuration management	A discipline, normally supported by software tools, that gives management precise control over its assets (for example, the products of a project), covering identification, control, status accounting and verification of the products.
Configuration status account	A report on the status of products in the configuration library.
Contingency budget	An amount of money required to cover a contingency plan, which is a plan ready in case a specific risk occurs. If the risk occurs the contingency budget would be called upon in order to implement the contingency plan. The Project Board must approve the plan and budget when the risk is analysed.
Contingency plan	A plan that provides an outline of decisions and measures to be taken if a defined risk should occur.
Critical path	This is the line connecting the start of a planning network with the final activity in the network of the project for achieving the earliest possible delivery. Often this is a line through the network connecting those activities with a zero float, i.e. those activities where any delay will delay the time of product delivery.
Customer	The person or group who commissioned the work and will benefit from the end results.
End Project Report	A report given by the Project Manager to the Project Board, which confirms the hand-over of all deliverables and provides an updated Business Case and an assessment of how well the project has done against its Project Initiation Document.
End stage assessment	The review by the Project Board and Project Manager of the End Stage Report to decide whether to approve the next Stage Plan (unless the last stage has now been completed). According to the size and criticality of the project, the review may be formal or informal. The approval to proceed should be documented as an important management product.
End Stage Report	A report given by the Project Manager to the Project Board at the end of each management stage of the project. This provides information about the project performance during the stage and the project status at stage end.
Exception	A situation where it can be forecast that there will be a deviation beyond the tolerances agreed between the Project Manager and Project Board (or between the Project Board and corporate or programme management, or between a Team Manager and the Project Manager).
Exception assessment	An Exception assessment is an assessment by the Project Board of an Exception Plan.
Exception Plan	This is a plan that often follows an Exception Report. For a Stage Plan exception, it covers the period from the present to the end of the current stage. If the exception were at a project level, the Project Plan would be replaced.

Exception Report	A report that describes a forecast deviation beyond a tolerance, provides an analysis and options for the way forward, and identifies a recommended option. The Project Manager presents it to the Project Board.
Executive	The chairperson of the Project Board, representing the customer.
Feasibility study	A feasibility study is a study of a problem in which alternative solutions are developed for the problem and in which the viability (being the main points in the Business Case) of these different options is examined.
Follow-on Action Recommendations	A report that can be used as input for a Business Case or Project Mandate for any follow-on project or for recording any follow-on instructions covering incomplete products or outstanding issues. It also sets out proposals for a post-project review of the project's products.
Gantt chart	This is a diagram of a plan's activities against a time background, showing start and end times and resources required.
Highlight Report	A periodical report from the Project Manager to the Project Board on stage progress.
Issue Log	A log of all Project Issues including requests for change raised during the project, showing details of each issue, its evaluation, what decisions have been made about it and its current status.
Lessons Learned Report	A report that describes the lessons learned during the project including statistics from quality control of the project's management products. It is approved by the Project Board and then held centrally for the benefit of future projects.
Off-specification	Something that should be provided by the project, but currently is not (or is forecast not to be) provided. This might be a missing product or a product not meeting its specification.
Outcome	The product or service the project is set up to deliver.
Post-implementation review	See Post-project review.
Post-project review	One or more reviews held after project closure to determine if the expected benefits have been obtained.
PRINCE2	A method that supports some selected aspects of project management. The acronym stands for PRojects IN Controlled Environments.
PRINCE2 project	A project whose product(s) can be defined at its start sufficiently precisely so as to be measurable against predefined metrics and that is managed according to PRINCE2 method.
Process	That which must be done to bring about a particular outcome, in terms of information to be gathered, decisions to be made, and results that must be achieved.
Producer	This role represents the creator(s) of a product that is the subject of a quality review. Typically it will be filled by the person who has produced the product, or who has led the team responsible.

Product	Any input to or output from a project. PRINCE2 distinguishes between management products (which are produced as part of the management of the project) and specialist products (which are those products that make up the final deliverable). A product may itself be a collection of other products.
Product-based planning	A three-step diagrammatic technique leading to a comprehensive plan based on creation and delivery of required products.
Product Checklist	A list of the major products of a plan, plus key dates in their delivery.
Product Description	A description of a product's purpose, composition, derivation and quality criteria. It is produced at planning time, as soon as the need for the product is identified.
Product Flow Diagram	A diagram showing the sequence of production and interdependencies of the products listed in a Product Breakdown Structure.
Programme	A programme is the entirety of projects and activities in a temporary organisation for the purpose of developing one or more business objectives that have been defined in advance.
Project	A temporary organisation that is created for the purpose of delivering one or more business products according to a specified Business Case.
Project Assurance	The Project Board's responsibilities to assure itself that the project is being conducted correctly.
Project Brief	A description of what the project is to do; a refined and extended version of the Project Mandate, which has been agreed by the Project Board and which is input to project initiation.
Project closure notification	Advice from the Project Board to inform the host organisation that the team members and support services such as space, equipment and access are no longer needed.
Project closure recommendation	Notification prepared by the Project Manager for the Project Board to send (when the board is satisfied that the project can be closed) to any organisation that has supplied facilities to the project.
Project Initiation Document (PID)	A logical document that brings together the key information needed to start the project on a sound basis and to convey that information to all concerned with the project.
Project Issue	A term used to cover general issues such as Requests for Change. Project Issues can be about anything to do with the project such as a query, Requests for Change, and off-specification.
Project Management	All management tasks required such as organising, planning, monitoring and control of all aspects of the project and the motivation of all this involved in it to achieve the project objectives.
Project Management Team	A term to represent the entire management structure of Project Board, Project Manager, plus any Team Managers, Project Assurance and project Support roles.

Project Manager	The person given the authority and responsibility to manage the project on a day-to-day basis to deliver the required products within the constraints agreed with the Project Board.
Project Mandate	Information created externally to the project, which forms the terms of reference and is used to start up the PRINCE2 project.
Project owner	Is not a PRINCE2 term, but is used in many organisations and is equivalent to Executive.
Project Plan	A high-level plan showing the major products of the project, when they will be delivered and at what cost. An initial Project Plan is presented as part of the Project Initiation Document. This is revised as information of actual project progress appears.
Project Quality Plan	A plan defining the key quality criteria, quality control and audit processes to be applied to project management and specialist work in the PRINCE2 project. It will be a part of the Project Initiation Document.
Project start-up notification	Advice to the host location that the project is about to start and requesting any required Project Support services.
Project Support Office	A group set up to provide certain administrative services to the Project Manager. Often the group provides its services to many projects in parallel.
Quality	The totality of features and characteristics of a product or service that bear on its ability to satisfy stated and implied needs.
Quality Management System	All quality standards, procedures and responsibilities for a site or organisation.
Quality review	A Quality review is a quality-checking technique with a specific structure, defined roles and procedure designed to ensure a product's completeness and adherence to standards. The participants are drawn from those with an interest in the product and those with the necessary skills to review its correctness.
Request for Change	A means of proposing a modification to the current specification of a product. It is one type of Project Issue.
Risk Log	A document that provides identification, estimation, impact evaluation and counter measures for all risks to the project. It should be created during the start-up of the project and developed during the life of the project.
Risk profile	A graphical representation of the possibility and impact of a risk. The risk profile of individual risks are normally found on the Risk Log.
Senior Supplier	The Project Board role that is responsible for providing the knowledge, resources and experience needed to achieve the project results.
Senior User	A member of the Project Board, accountable for ensuring that user needs are specified correctly and that the project outcome meets those needs.

Specialist Product

A product that has to be made during the project as part of the specifications. It may be part of the outcome or a semi-finished product, on which one or more subsequent product depends.

Sponsor

Not a PRINCE2 term, but is often used in organisation to mean the major driving force of a project. The sponsor may be the Executive or a representative of corporate or programme management.

Stage

A time-driven section of the project with activities and deliverables defined in advance.

Stakeholders

Parties with an interest in the execution and outcome of a project.

Supplier

The person or group responsible for the supply of the project's specialist products.

Team Manager

The person responsible for developing the specialist products, according to the agreed Work Package.

Tolerance

The permissible deviation above and below a plan's estimate of time, costs, scope, quality, risks, benefits and changes to a project. Deviations within the tolerance limits do not need escalating to the next level of management.

User

The person or group who will use the final deliverable(s) of the project.

Work Package

The comprehensive group of specialist products and the information relevant to the creation of these products. The information includes the Product Descriptions, constraints such as time and budget, dependencies and confirmation of the agreement between the Project Manager and the person or Team Manager who is to implement the products within the constraints.

7.2 Management products

In this description of the management products, the Exception Plan is dealt with under the description of the Stage Plan and the Issue Log is dealt with under the description of the Project Issue.

7.2.1 Acceptance Criteria

Purpose:

Acceptance Criteria are measurable requirements that the deliverables must meet. These measurable requirements must ensure that the conditions under which the customer will accept the deliverables are clear.

Composition:

Acceptance Criteria differ for each type of deliverable. Acceptance Criteria may contain values for:
- Delivery dates
- Major functions
- Form
- Required commitment by staff/cost of management and maintenance
- Performance levels
- Capacity
- Accuracy
- Availability
- User friendliness
- Flexibility
- Reliability
- Investment costs
- Security

Derivation:
- Senior User
- Corporate or programme management
- Customer's quality expectations

The Acceptance Criteria are part of the Project Brief and are recorded for the first time in the subprocess Preparing a Project Brief (SU4). The Acceptance Criteria are set out in more detail in the Project Quality Plan during the subprocess Planning Quality (IP1).

Quality criteria:
- Are all criteria measurable?
- Are all criteria individually feasible?
- Are all criteria jointly feasible?
- Does an outcome that meets all the criteria deliver a product that is acceptable to the customer?

7.2.2 Business Case

Purpose:

The Business Case gives the practical justification for the project. The Business Case answers the questions: why are we doing this project? Which investments will be needed? What will the Executive achieve with the outcome? The Business Case will be tested at set periods during the project to make sure that the ultimate outcome remains valid for the customer.

Composition:
- Background, reasons for starting the project:
  - Connection with corporate objectives
- Possible options that have been considered
- Expected benefits to the organisation (customer)
- Major risks
- Cost (extract from Project Plan)
- Timescales (extract from Project Plan)
- Investment appraisal (return on investment)

Derivation:
- Customer's corporate or programme management
- Project Mandate
- Project Plan
- Risk Log

The reasons for undertaking the project are given in the Project Mandate. The process Starting Up a Project looks at whether there is already a Business Case for the project and the outline of the Business Case is defined (SU4). The Business Case is refined in the Initiation Stage (IP3). The Initial Business Case is part of the PID. The Business Case is updated throughout the lifecycle of the project.

Quality criteria:
- Is the Business Case in line with corporate objectives and the strategy of the organisation?
- Can the benefits be supported?
- Does the Business Case fit in with the Project Plan?
- Have the relevant risks in the Risk Log been incorporated into the Business Case?

7.2.3 Checkpoint Report

Purpose:

The Checkpoint Report is a periodic report from the Team Manager to the Project Manager about the progress and status of the activities and of the interim and other results of the Work Package that the Team Manager has to deliver.

Composition:
- Date
- Period
- Status of action points from the previous period
- Activities in the previous period, plus current status
- Products completed during the previous period, plus current status
- Quality checks carried out in the previous period
- Spending in the previous period, plus current status
- Actual or potential problems and status of risks
- Impact of changes on costs and scheduling
- Work for the next period
- Products to be completed in the next period

Derivation:
- Verbal reports by the Team Managers
- Stage and Team Plans
- Previous Checkpoint Reports

The Checkpoint Reports are written in the subprocess Executing a Work Package (MP2).

Quality criteria:
- Are there reports on all the relevant components in the Stage and Team Plans in question?
- Are all members of the team working according to the agreed team plans?
- Are there reports on all the outstanding Project Issues from the previous report?

7.2.4 Communication Plan

Purpose:

This plan is the means for recording all forms of communication from and to the stakeholders. In this way, all interested parties gain insight into the way in which, and with which frequency, communication takes place between them and the project.

Composition:
- Target groups
- Which information is required?
- Who provides the information?
- When is which information given?
- Which method of communication is used for issuing information?

Derivation:
- Project Board
- Project Brief
- Project Approach
- Project Plan

The Communication Plan is written in the subprocess Setting up Project Controls (IP4).

Quality criteria:
- Have all the stakeholders been identified and have their communication needs been taken into account?
- Has agreement been reached with all stakeholders with regard to content, frequency and manner of communication?
- Has two-way traffic been set up for communication?
- Have the various communication means and frequencies been brought into line?
- Are there provisions for time, cost and capacity for undertaking communication activities?
- Are there provisions for a review of whether the manner of communication is effective?

7.2.5 Configuration Item Record

Purpose:

The Configuration Item Record contains information about a product (configuration item) that can be used to clearly establish the status of that product, including interfaces with other products.

Composition:

- Mandatory:
  - Project number
  - Product Description
  - Product identification number
  - Version
  - Status
- Optional:
  - Owner
  - Author
  - Copy holders
  - Date (latest status change)
  - Location
  - Historical summary: previous versions, dates, reasons for change
  - Product Description
  - Source (in-house or purchased from a third party)
  - Development stages to go through
  - Related products
  - Reference to approved Requests for Change
  - Reference to relevant correspondence

Document status information is often included at the back of the document.

Derivation:

- Product Breakdown Structure
- Stage Plans and Team Plans
- Work Packages
- Quality Log
- Change control

Configuration Item Records are recorded in the configuration management database that is created as part of the Configuration Management Plan in the subprocess Setting up Project Files (IP5).

Quality criteria:

- Does the Configuration Item show the correct status of the product?
- Are all Configuration Items stored correctly in the configuration management database and is this secure enough?
- Does the version number of the Configuration Item match the products in circulation?
- Have the Configuration Items copyholders received the relevant copies?
- Have changes to the status of the Configuration Items been authorised and have these authorised changes been recorded?

7.2.6 Configuration Management Plan

Purpose:
To create a clear, structured record of how products are managed in a project.

Composition:
- Objective of configuration management
- Configuration management method used
- Reference to any other relevant configuration management systems in use
- How and where configuration items are stored (e.g. the directory structure)
- Procedures for receiving and issuing configuration items
- Product and document coding structure
- Who is responsible for configuration management

Derivation:
- Customer's quality management system and that of the supplier
- Specific requirements with regard to products to be used and developed in the project
- Project organisation structure
- Required configuration management software

The Configuration Management Plan is written as part of the Project Quality Plan in the subprocess Planning Quality (IP1). The project files, which are part of the Configuration Management Plan, are established in the subprocess Setting up Project Files (IP5).

Quality criteria:
- Are the responsibilities clear to both the customer and the supplier?
- Has the product and document coding structure been established?
- Are the agreements on version control and for issue and distribution clear?
- Have provisions been made for all stakeholders to receive information relevant to them?

7.2.7 Daily Log

Purpose:

To create a structured record of all the relevant information and events in the project that are not, or not fully, covered by other documents. The Daily Log can be an effective control mechanism for both the Project Manager and the Team Manager. The Daily Log often functions as the personal log of the person keeping it. In certain sectors the Daily Log may be a contractual commitment between parties.

Composition:
- Date of registration
- Action/observation
- Person responsible
- Planned completion date
- Result

Derivation:
- Risk Log
- Stage Plan
- Checkpoint Report
- Quality Log
- Conversations, meetings and observations

The Daily Log is set up during the subprocess Setting up Project Files (IP5). Registration in the Daily Log can take place in all the subsequent processes during the implementation of the project, but particularly during the process Controlling a Stage.

Quality criteria:
- Are the notes in the log legible and clear/comprehensible for someone consulting it at a later date?
- Have all the relevant notes been used for statements in the management products intended for this?
- Has the date, the person responsible and the planned completion date been filled in as required?

7.2.8 End Project Report

Purpose:

The Project Manager uses this report at the end of the project to account for the course of the project to the Project Board. In the report, the delivered outcome is compared with the desired outcome as recorded in the Project Initiation Document. The End Project Report includes a list of the total cost, the schedule, tolerances, the most up-to-date and approved Business Case and the Project Plan.

Composition:
- Project outcome (deliverables, time, money)
- Comparison of the project outcome with the initial Project Plan
- Effect of approved changes on the original Project Plan and initial Business Case
- Summary of Project Issues
- Impact of approved Requests for Change
- Summary of quality checks
- Post Project Review Plan (including dates)

Derivation:
- The updated Project Plan (including the Stage Plan, Exception Plan and team plans)
- Risk Log
- Issue Log
- Quality Log
- Lessons Learned Report
- End Stage Report(s)
- PID

The End Project Report is written in the subprocess Evaluating a Project (CP3).

Quality criteria:
- Does the report describe the consequences of the approved changes on the PID?
- Does the report contain all the benefits that can be assessed when the project is delivered?
- Does the report give a good account of the course of the project?
- Is everyone who is responsible for Project Assurance in agreement with the content of the report?

7.2.9 End Stage Report

Purpose:

The End Stage Report gives an insight into the progress and current status of the project and is an account by the Project Manager of the outcome and execution of the stage just ended. It provides the Project Board with information on which it can make well-founded decisions about continuing with the project and can release the Project Manager from the current stage.

Composition:
- Status of current Stage Plan (updated)
- Status of Project Plan (updated)
- Status of Business Case (updated)
- Status of risks (updated)
- Overview of Project Issues
- Overview of quality checks carried out
- Account by Project Manager

Derivation:
- Current Stage Plan with the actual status of the stage
- Stage Plan for the next stage or Exception Plan (if applicable)
- Project Plan
- Business Case
- Risk Log
- Configuration management database with the Configuration Items Records
- Lessons Learned Log
- Quality Log
- Issue Log

The End Stage Report is written in the subprocess Reporting Stage End (SB5) of the process Managing Stage Boundaries.

Quality criteria:
- Does the report give a clear picture of progress versus the plan?
- Does the report give a good account of the stage just completed?
- Does the report give a good picture of how the project should continue and the technical and practical feasibility of the project?
- Is everyone who is responsible for Project Assurance in agreement about the content of the report?

7.2.10 Exception Report

Purpose:

An Exception Report is written when the agreed tolerances risk being exceeded. The Project Manager writes the Exception Report as a means of informing the Project Board. The Project Board must respond to the Exception Report. The most probable response is to ask the Project Manager to make an Exception Plan to replace the current plan.

Composition:
- Description of the cause of a deviation
- Consequences of a deviation
- Available options, showing for each option the consequences for the following:
  - Business Case
  - Risks
  - Current Project Plan
  - Current Stage Plan
- The Project Manager's recommendations

Derivation:
- The current up-to-date Stage Plan
- Business Case
- Issue Log
- Risk Log
- Project Plan
- PID
- Advice from the Project Board on external events that could affect the project

The Exception Report is written in the subprocess Escalating Project Issues (CS8), if there is a danger that the stage tolerances will be exceeded.

Quality criteria:
- Is there an indication of the cause of the exception?
- Is there a clear indication in the current Stage Plan of the current status of the project?
- Have the aspects time, money, quality, scope (reach) and technical feasibility been included in the description of the consequences for the Stage Plan and the Project Plan, as well as the consequences for other parts of the project?
- Does the Project Manager's recommendation include the information on which this is based?

7.2.11 Follow-On Action Recommendations

Purpose:

To be a structured record of all the relevant recommendations for the stage in which the product is to be used, to be able to transfer it to the relevant organisation. This leads to:

- A good transfer of the outcome to the users
- The users' acceptance of the outcome
- The chance that the anticipated benefits that the customer expects to get from the outcome will actually be achieved

Composition:

- Date of report
- Recommendations as a result of submitted Requests for Change
- Recommendations as a result of Off-Specifications
- Recommendations as a result of risks identified which may affect the product in its operational life
- Recommendations with regard to handing-over the outcome
- Recommendations with regard to necessary training
- Other recommendations relevant to the stage in which the product is to be used

Derivation:

- Issue Log
- Risk Log
- Quality Log
- Lessons Learned Log

The Follow-On Action Recommendations will be drawn up in the subprocess Identifying Follow-On Actions (CP2).

Quality criteria:

- Have recommendations been defined with regard to all the outstanding Project Issues?
- Have all outstanding Project Issues been closed with an entry to signify that they have been transferred to these recommendations?
- Has all the relevant documentation been attached to the recommendations?

7.2.12 Highlight Report

Purpose:

The Project Manager writes the Highlight Report for the Project Board to give the members a periodical summary of the status and progress of the project.

Composition:
- Issue date
- Period
- Budget report
- Checkpoint Report
- Products developed in the last period
- Actual or potential problems and the status of risks
- Products to be completed in the next period
- Project Issues status
- Budget and schedule impact of any changes

Derivation:
- Stage Plan or Exception Plan
- Checkpoint Reports and progress meetings
- Risk Log
- Issue Log
- Quality Log
- Communication Plan

The Highlight Report is written in the subprocess Reporting Highlights (CS6).

Quality criteria:
- Does the report show the correct current status of the stage?
- Are the relevant Project Issues and risks shown correctly and in full?
- Is the report concise and suitable for information to and assessment by the recipients?

7.2.13 Lessons Learned Log

Purpose:
To keep a structured record of the lessons learned during a project. These lessons learned may be useful for a next project or project stage.

Composition:
- Causes of deviations to plan
- Lessons learned about quality and management processes
  - What went well, what could be done better, recommendations
- Lessons learned about specialist methods, techniques and tools
  - What went well, what could be done better, recommendations
- Lessons learned about quality assessments (reviews and tests)
  - What went well, what could be done better, recommendations
- Costing activities

Derivation:
- Quality Log
- Risk Log
- Completed Work Packages
- Highlight Reports
- Checkpoint Reports
- Updated Stage Plans
- General observations and experiences throughout the project

The Lessons Learned Log is set up during the subprocess Setting up Project Files (IP5). Lessons learned can be recorded in the Lessons Learned Log at any time in the project. The lessons learned should be reviewed and the lessons learned recorded in the Lessons Learned Report at every stage boundary (in the subprocess SB5).

Quality criteria:
- Have all the control mechanisms been included in the assessment?
- Have the reasons for all deviations from the agreed tolerances been recorded?
- Were the people responsible for Project Assurance, the Team Managers, the Team members and the members of Project Support involved in the review?
- Has the Lessons Learned Log been updated at least at the end of every stage?
- Are the results of the quality assessments included in the log?

7.2.14 Lessons Learned Report

Purpose:

To be a structured record of the lessons learned at the end of the project so that all the relevant lessons learned in the project can be passed on to the organisations involved.

Composition:
- Causes of deviations from plan
- Lessons learned about quality and management processes
  - What went well, what could be done better, recommendations
- Lessons learned about specialist methods, techniques and tools
  - What went well, what could be done better, recommendations
- Statistical review of quality assessments
- Costing activities

Derivation:
- Lessons Learned Log
- End of Stage reports
- Quality Log

The Lessons Learned Report is compiled in the subprocess Identifying Follow-On Actions (CP2) at the end of the project.

Quality criteria:
- Have all control mechanisms been included in the review?
- Has a statistical review of the extent to which the quality assessments were successful been included in the review: how many errors were found after products had been approved?
- Has costing data for production, quality and management products been included?

7.2.15 Off-Specification

Purpose:

To be a structured record of a situation or of a product that does not or will not meet the Acceptance Criteria specified so that work can be done on correcting the (consequences of) exceptions in a controlled manner.

Composition:
- Reference number
- Date of registration
- Type of Project Issue (Off-Specification)
- Status
- Description of the fault
- Impact of the fault
- Priority
- Decision (plus name and signature of person with the power of decision)
- Corrective measures (plus who is responsible and when it should be ready)
- Decision date
- Completion date

Derivation:

Anyone may bring up an Off-Specification. The Off-Specification is recorded as a Project Issue in the subprocess Capturing Project Issues (CS3). The impact of the deviation is examined in the subprocess Examining Project Issues (CS4) and possible corrective action is defined.

Quality criteria:
- Have all Off-Specifications been recorded in the Issue Log?
- Are the Off-Specifications well described?
- Has the SMART (Specific, Measurable, Acceptable, Realistic and Time-related) corrective action been described and is there a record of who is responsible for carrying out the corrective measures?

7.2.16 Post Project Review Plan

Purpose:

To be a structured record of how and when it can be determined whether the customer has achieved the benefits he wanted to achieve with the project outcome.

Composition:
- How to measure achievement of the expected benefits
- When the benefits can be measured
- Required commitment of people and resources

Derivation:
- Business Case
- Discussions with end users and those involved with management and maintenance

The Post Project Review Plan is drawn up in the subprocess Identifying Follow-On Actions (CP2) at the end of the project.

Quality criteria:
- Are all the expected benefits included in the review?
- Is the review not being done too soon after delivery or, alternatively, in the too distant future?
- Are the right people involved in the review?
- Is the commitment of people and resources needed for the review proportionate to the size of the expected benefits?

7.2.17 Product Breakdown Structure

Purpose:

To be a structured record of all products that have to be developed or that are needed in the project for delivery of the project outcome.

Composition:

A hierarchical classification of all the products that are to be developed:
- Specialist products
  - Interim products
  - End products
  - External products
- Management products
  - Quality products
  - Other management products

Derivation:
- Project Brief
- Project Quality Plan
- Users and project team members involved
- Those who are responsible for Project Assurance

The Product Breakdown Structure is set up or updated in the subprocess Defining and Analysing Products (PL2). This happens each time a plan has to be made.

Quality criteria:
- Do the products deliver what the customer will need at a later date to achieve the desired benefits?
- Has the breakdown been clearly identified and distinguished to be able to monitor the progress of the work?
- Can Product Descriptions for the bottom level of breakdown be written without further decomposition?
- Have all the external products that are needed to be able to achieve the final outcome been included in the breakdown?
- Are there provisions for a review to actually test these external products on their required quality before they are used in the project?
- Have all the relevant quality products been included in the breakdown as they are described in the Project Quality Plan (for example, 'test plans to be set up')?
- Have all the other relevant management products also been included in the breakdown?
- Is the numbering and are the names of all the products in the breakdown unique?
- Does the bottom level of the breakdown match the products in the Product Flow Diagram one-on-one?
- Is the breakdown hierarchical (no products that are part of an itemisation of more than one higher product, no one-on-one breakdown)?
- Have the compound products that are to be reviewed also been included in the bottom level of breakdown?
- Have the interim products needed to be able to deliver the final project outcome been included in the breakdown?

7.2.18 Product Checklist

Purpose:

To be a structured record of all the products that have to be developed in a plan period (with the most important plan dates), so that management can monitor the progress of the work easily.

Composition:
- Plan identification
- Products to be developed, including their products codes, if any
- Planned and actual dates:
  - Start date
  - Date draft is ready
  - Date of quality check
  - Date of final approval

Derivation:
- Product Breakdown Structure
- Schedule

The Product Checklist is drawn up in the subprocess Defining and Analysing Products (PL2). The list is completed with the plan dates in the subprocess Completing a Plan (PL7). The actual accomplished dates will be included during the progress of the work.

Quality criteria:
- Do the products correspond to the bottom level of the Product Breakdown Structure?
- Do the planned dates correspond to the relevant plan?
- Are there separate dates filled in for draft, review and delivery?

7.2.19 Product Description

Purpose:

The purpose of writing a Product Description is to ensure that all the stakeholder parties have the same idea of the product to be developed, the requirements the product must meet, and how and by whom the product must be approved.

Composition:
- Identifier
- Name of the product
- Purpose of the product
- Composition
- Derivation (sources)
- Format and presentation
- Person responsible for development
- Quality criteria
- Type of quality check
- Responsibilities or knowledge and skills needed for quality check

Derivation:
- Product Breakdown Structure
- Users
- Customer or supplier's current quality system

A Product Description must be written as soon as the product is found to be a necessary part of the project. The Product Description is frozen as soon as the plan that includes the development of the product has been approved.

Quality criteria:
- Is it clear why the product is needed?
- Is the Product Description sufficiently detailed to be able to write a good plan for developing the product and to be able to monitor the development progress?
- Is it clear who is responsible for the development of the product?
- Are the quality criteria consistent and measurable and do the criteria correspond to the applicable quality standards and the agreed Acceptance Criteria?
- Can this type of quality check determine whether the quality criteria have been met?
- Has the Product Description been written by people with sufficient knowledge of the product to be developed?

7.2.20 Product Flow Diagram

Purpose:
To be a structured record of the logical sequence and the dependencies between the products to be developed and the external products, in order for a good basis to be developed so that the activities to be undertaken can be specified and the final plan can be drawn up.

Composition:
A flow diagram showing all the products to be developed:
• Specialist products
• Management products

Derivation:
• Product Breakdown Structure
• Product Descriptions

The Flow Diagrams are designed in the individual plans in the subprocess Defining and Analysing Products (PL2). This is done in conjunction with the Product Breakdown Structure and the Product Descriptions.

Quality criteria:
• Have all the products been included one-on-one in the flow diagram at the bottom level of the Product Breakdown Structure?
• Are the products that have been included sufficient to deliver the project outcome and does this also deliver what the customer needs to achieve the desired benefits at a later date?
• Have all the external products needed to be able to achieve the final outcome been included in the flow diagram?
• Have the relevant quality products and the other relevant management products been included? Does this correspond to what has been included in the Product Breakdown Structure?
• Are all the descriptions of the products identical to the descriptions in the Product Breakdown Structure?
• Are all the products, with the exception of the start and end product, related to at least one other product both at the beginning and at the end?
• Do the defined relationships in the flow diagram match the relationships in the Product Descriptions?
• Is the flow diagram drawn from top to bottom or from right to left?
• Are there any 'loops' in the flow diagram?

7.2.21 Project Approach

Purpose:

To act as a structured record of the way in which the project outcome is to be achieved. Agreement must be reached with the management of the project on this before the project is begun.

Composition:
- Description of the approach
- Reasons for the approach

Possible ways of achieving the project outcome are:
- Own development versus outsourcing?
- Adapt existing product or make new one?
- Own staff and/or contractors?
- Standard or customised?
- Fixed price or time and materials?

Derivation:
- Corporate or programme management
- Project Brief
- Person responsible for design
- Senior Supplier
- Market

The Project Approach is laid down in the subprocess Defining Project Approach (SU5).

Quality criteria:
- Can the project outcome be delivered by means of the chosen approach, within the constraints of time, money and quality?
- When choosing the approach was account taken of the expertise and capabilities of those who have to accomplish the project outcome?
- Is the Project Approach in line with the future production and management environment?
- Are the project and business risks acceptable and manageable?

7.2.22 Project Brief

Purpose:

The Project Brief enables the Project Board and the corporate or programme management to check whether the project is sufficiently viable to start the process Initiating a Project. The Project Brief is also the basis for writing the PID.

Composition:
- Background:
  - Context of the project
  - Reason for starting the project
- Project definition:
  - Project objectives
  - Scope (reach)
  - Most important project deliverables or outcomes
  - Any exclusions
  - Constraints
  - Interfaces with other projects
- Outline of Business Case:
  - A description of the way in which the outcome of this project contributes to business objectives or strategies
  - Why this project has been chosen
- Customer's quality expectations
- Acceptance criteria
- Known risks
- Outline of Project Plan (if known)

Derivation:
- Project Mandate
- Information from corporate or programme management
- Information from all other parties involved in the project

The Project Brief is developed in the process Starting Up a Project.

Quality criteria:
- Is the Project Brief in line with the Project Mandate?
- Does the Project Brief give a good, comprehensive picture of the project?
- Does the Project Brief provide management with sufficient basis to establish whether the project is valid and to authorise project initiation?
- Is the Project Brief a good basis for writing the PID?
- Is it clear when the Executive will be satisfied with the final outcome?

7.2.23 Project Initiation Document (PID)

Purpose:

The Project Initiation Document contains all the information necessary for the Project Board to be able to authorise the implementation of the project. It is the basis for managing the project.

Composition:

- Stable part
  - Background:
    - Context of the project
    - Reasons for starting the project
  - Project definition:
    - Project objectives
    - Project approach
    - Project scope
    - Most important project outcome
    - Exclusions
    - Constraints
    - Interfaces with other projects
    - Assumptions
  - Project organisation structure:
    - Project management structure
    - Job descriptions (tasks, responsibilities, powers)
  - Communication Plan
  - Project Quality Plan
  - Controls
- Dynamic part
  - Initial Business Case
  - Initial Project Plan
  - Initial Risk Log

Derivation:

- Supplier's project management standard
- Customer's specified control requirements
- Project Mandate and Project Brief
- All the documents drawn up during the process Initiating a Project

The PID is drawn up as the last part of the process Initiating a Project. Following approval by the Project Board, the document itself will no longer be changed. Parts of the PID may however be updated, in particular Business Case, the Project Plan and the Risk Log.

Quality criteria:

- Does the document give a good and complete picture of the project?
- Does the document describe a valid and feasible project that is in line with the objectives of corporate or programme management?
- Is the project management team structure complete and have all the roles and associated tasks, responsibilities and powers been filled in?
- Does the report show a clear reporting and consultation structure and is this suitable for directing the project well?
- Are the agreed controls suitable for those who are responsible for Project Assurance?
- Is it clear who is responsible for recording the various controls and keeping them up to date?

7.2.24 Project Issue and Issue Log

Purpose:

All Project Issues and the actions to be taken as a result of these must be clearly recorded in a project. Each Project Issue is registered by type, status and consequences. All the Project Issues are registered in the Issue Log.

Subjects for Project Issue:
- Reference number
- Date of registration
- Type of Project Issue (Request for Change, Off-Specification or General)
- Author
- Description
- Status
- Impact
- Priority
- Decision (plus name and signature of the person authorised to make decisions)
- Actions (plus who is responsible for them)
- Date of decision
- Date completed

Subjects for Issue Log:
- Reference number
- Date of registration
- Type of Project Issue (Request for Change, Off-Specification or General)
- Person submitting it
- Description
- Status
- Priority
- Decision
- Date of last update

Derivation:

The Issue Log is set up in the subprocess Setting up Project Files (IP5). The Issue Log is updated every time new Project Issues are registered or the status of existing Project Issues changes.

Anyone can submit a Project Issue. How to register Project Issues is described in the subprocess CS3. The review of Project Issues is described in the subprocess CS4.

Quality criteria:
- Is the problem, the question or the point for attention clear?
- Have all the consequences been considered when reviewing the Project Issues?
- Has the Project Issue been registered correctly?

7.2.25 Project Mandate

Purpose:

The information from the Project Mandate is needed to start the process Starting Up a Project. It should provide an insight into what the project amounts to and should at least contain enough information to be able to appoint the Executive of the project.

Composition:
- Responsible sponsor
- Background
- Objective
- Scope
- Constraints
- Interfaces with other projects
- Quality expectations
- Reasons for starting the project (outline of Business Case)
- Reference material
- Proposal for appointment of Executive and Project Manager
- Users and other stakeholders

Derivation:

The Project Mandate can be written by a number of parties in the customer organisation. The Project Mandate must however be released by the customer's corporate or programme management that has the power to authorise spending and deployment of people and resources. The Project Mandate is input for the process Starting Up a Project (SU).

Quality criteria:
- Has the Project Mandate been released by someone who has sufficient authority to do so?
- Is the Project Mandate sufficient for deciding on and appointing the most suitable Executive and Project Manager?
- Have all the stakeholders in the project been identified?
- Does the Project Mandate show what the project involves at management level and what the customer wishes to accomplish?

7.2.26 Project Plan

Purpose:

As part of the Project Initiation Document, the Project Plan is a broad outline plan of the project describing how, by whom and when the objectives of the project will be achieved. It gives an insight into the people and resources that are needed and at what cost. It provides the Business Case with information about the planned costs, time and the products to be developed. It serves as a basic document that the Project Board can use to test progress and costs in each stage.

Composition:

- Description of the plan including scope
- Project conditions: what has to be ready or arranged before implementation can begin?
- External dependencies
- Planning assumptions
- Graphic representation of:
  - Product Breakdown Structure
  - Product Flow Diagram
  - Product Descriptions
  - Activity network
  - Scheduling (for example in the form of a Gantt chart)
  - Required people and resources
  - Project budget
  - Change budget
  - Project tolerances (time and money at least)
  - Contingency plan if relevant

Derivation:

- Project Brief
- Project Approach
- Project Quality Plan

The Project Plan is drawn up in the subprocess Planning a Project (IP2).

Quality criteria:

- Is the plan realistic?
- Does the plan give a good description of the project?
- Can the Project Board use the plan to direct the project?
- Is the plan a good basis for the other parts of the PID?

7.2.27 Project Quality Plan

Purpose:

The Project Quality Plan is part of the Project Initiation Document. This plan contains descriptions of how the quality of the products to be developed in the project can be assured so that the customer's quality expectations can be met (according to agreed quality standards).

Composition:
- Customer's quality expectations
- Acceptance criteria
- Those responsible for quality
- Applicable quality standards
- Quality management system with respect to:
  - Project management
  - Specialists' work
- Change procedure
- Configuration Management Plan
- Quality methods and techniques to be applied (for example, quality reviews or certain types of tests)

Derivation:
- Project Brief
- Project Approach
- Customer's quality management system and that of the supplier
- Requirements with regard to configuration management
- Requirements with regard to the change procedure to be used

The Project Quality Plan is drawn up in the subprocess IP1.

Quality criteria:
- Are the defined procedures sufficient to meet the customer's quality expectations?
- Have the responsibilities for achieving the required quality been clearly defined?
- Have the responsibilities for quality also been defined to a level beyond the project?
- Does the plan conform to the quality policy of the organisations involved?

7.2.28 Quality Log

Purpose:

The Quality Log gives a clear and central record of:

- All products that have to be tested
- How the products have to be tested
- When the results of the tests have to be delivered and the corrective action to be taken

Composition:

- Reference number
- Product
- Quality check:
  - Type
  - Person responsible
  - Date planned
  - Actual date
  - Result
- Agreed action (when, by whom)
- Planned approval date
- Approval date

Derivation:

The Stage Plan contains the list of products that have to be evaluated, when and how, and who is responsible for the review. The other information is added after the quality assessment has been carried out. The actual approval date is added after all corrective action has actually been undertaken and signed in agreement.

Quality criteria:

- Is there a procedure that guarantees that all the quality assessments to be carried out are actually included in the Quality Log?
- Has the responsibility for keeping the Quality Log up-to-date been assigned to a specific person?

7.2.29 Request for Change

Purpose:

A Request for Change is a request to alter the current specification of a product. These requests may relate to products that still have to be developed or to products that have already been approved.

Composition:
- Issue Log reference number
- Date of registration
- Type of Project Issue (Request for Change)
- Status
- Description
- Impact
- Priority
- Decision (plus name and signature of person authorised to make decisions)
- Actions (plus who is responsible for what and when what has to be ready)
- Decision date
- Date completed

Derivation:

Anyone can submit a Request for Change. Users and project team members often bring up Project Issues. Many Requests for Change also result from quality reviews. Registering Requests for Change is described in the subprocess CS3 and assessing Requests for Change is described in the subprocess CS4 since Requests for Change are a specific type of Project Issue.

Quality criteria:
- Is it clear who submitted the Request for Change?
- Has the request been written clearly and unambiguously?
- Have the consequences in terms of time, money and quality been considered?
- Have the consequences for other parts of the project been considered?
- Have the possible benefits or effects on the forecast benefits been included in the assessment and can these benefits/effects be quantified?

7.2.30 Risk Log

Purpose:

This log is needed to record all the risk information centrally and unambiguously, including the risk analysis, the actual status and the countermeasures to be taken.

Composition:

- Risk identifier
- Date of registration
- Risk category (for example, commercial, technical, organisational, etc.)
- Description
- Effect if risks occur
- Chance of risks occurring
- Time span
- Countermeasures (prevention, reduction, transfer, acceptance, contingency plan)
- Risk owner
- Author
- Date of last update and list of decisions
- Status of the risk

Derivation:

The Risk Log is set up during the subprocess Preparing a Project Brief (OP4).

The Risk Log must be updated if new risks are identified and if the status of the risks is updated.

New risks can be identified:

- During the various risk analyses in the processes:
  - Starting Up a Project
  - Initiating a Project
  - Managing Stage Boundaries
- During the impact analysis for Project Issues
- Every time the Risk Log is consulted
- By the Project Board

Quality criteria:

- Does the Risk Log indicate which countermeasures have been taken or whether a contingency plan has been drawn up?
- Are the countermeasures and contingency plan included in the relevant Stage Plans?
- Does the Risk Log indicate how the risks are monitored, who the risk owners are and how the status of the risks is reported?
- Are these risk activities also included in the relevant Stage Plans?
- Have agreements been made about who has access to the Risk Log?

7.2.31 Stage Plan (or Exception Plan)

Purpose:

The Stage Plan for the current stage is the basis of the Project Manager's day-to-day management. The Stage Plan for the next stage is the basis on which the Project Board authorises the start of the next stage. The Exception Plan replaces the Stage Plan for the rest of the current stage after the Project Board has approved the Exception Plan.

Composition:
- Description of plan:
  - Scope
  - Approach
- Stage quality plan:
  - Quality checks to be used
  - People and resources required
- Plan prerequisites
- External dependencies
- Stage tolerances (in time and money at least)
- Controls
- Reporting
- Planning assumptions
- Graphic representation of:
  - Product Breakdown Structure
  - Product Flow Diagram
  - Activity network
  - Scheduling (e.g. in the form of a Gantt chart)
  - Required commitment of people and resources
  - Budget
  - Risk assessment
- Product Descriptions

Conditions for the plan show what has to be ready and arranged before the start. Product Descriptions of the most important deliverables in the stage have to be included.

The composition of the Exception Plan is the same as that of the Stage Plan, plus a copy of the corresponding Exception Report.

Derivation:
- Project Plan
- Current Stage Plan
- PID
- Risk Log
- Issue Log
- People and resource availability

The Stage Plan or Exception Plan is written in the process Managing Stage Boundaries. The Stage Plan is updated in the subprocess Assessing Progress (CS2) and if necessary altered in the subprocesses Reviewing Stage Status (CS5) and Taking Corrective Action (CS7).

Quality criteria:
- Is the plan complete and realistic?

- Do all the Team Managers who have to do the work in the plan agree with everything in their Work Packages?
- Does everyone responsible for Project Assurance agree with those parts of the plan relevant to them?
- Is the plan detailed enough to be able to manage the stage properly?
- Has the plan been drawn up in accordance with agreed guidelines?
- Is there provision in the plan for management activities?
- Have all the quality activities been included in the plan?

7.2.32 Work Package

Purpose:

This is the sum total of all the relevant information about one or more products collated by the Project Manager to pass responsibility for work on in a project to a Team Manager.

Composition:
- Date
- Person responsible for the work
- Work Package description
- Product Descriptions
- Interfaces to be developed with the deliverables
- Techniques, processes and procedures to be used
- Stage Plan outline
- Agreements about the start and end date, budget, commitment of people and resources
- Dependency on other activities
- Constraints
- Quality checks to be undertaken
- Agreements about independent quality checks
- Agreements regarding configuration management
- Agreements about the delivery (including the prior announcement)
- Agreements about hand-over of products after delivery
- Agreements about Checkpoint Reports
- Change control and escalation procedures

Derivation:
- Product Descriptions
- Stage Plans

Work Packages are put together in the subprocess Authorising Work Package (CS1).

Quality criteria:
- Is the Work Package SMART (Specific, Measurable, Acceptable, Realistic and Time-related)?
- Have Product Descriptions been defined for all the major deliverables in the Work Package?
- Has the required commitment of people and resources been agreed and are they available?
- Are the quality criteria clear and measurable, and has it been decided who is to undertake the various quality reviews and how?
- Have the above subjects in the Work Package been defined and agreed for as far as is relevant?

7.3 Health check

Before starting work on a project and during the course of a project it is a good idea to keep a finger on the pulse. Was the project started for the right reasons and is the current project still 'healthy'? The following list of questions can be used to establish whether the most important conditions are being met. The entire lifecycle of a project is checked like this.

7.3.1 Starting Up a Project

- Has the Executive delivered an approved Project Mandate?
- Are the reasons, the outcome and the objectives of the project clearly formulated in the Project Mandate?
- Has the project organisation been clearly defined and appointed?
- Have all the roles, tasks and responsibilities been clearly formulated?
- Has a Project Brief been written?
- Are the interfaces with other projects clearly described?
- Has the project been clearly and unambiguously defined and has the Executive established the exclusions?
- Is there a clear picture of the customer's quality expectations?
- Have the Acceptance Criteria for the various quality expectations been clearly established?
- Have the most important risks been identified and included in the Project Brief?
- Has an initial Risk Log been set up?
- Has the Project Approach been formulated clearly?
- Has a Stage Plan for the initiation stage been drawn up with a clear description of:
  - What has to be recorded?
  - Who has to do what and when?
  - How the documents to be delivered in the initiation stage are to be approved?
- Has the Project Board approved the Project Brief, the project organisation, the approach and the Initiation Stage Plan?
- Has the Project Board authorised the start of the initiation stage, and approved the required commitment of people and resources?
- Has the Project Board informed the organisations involved?

7.3.2 Initiating a Project

- Is there a complete and unambiguous specification of the demands placed on the project outcome?
- Is there a clear plan (quality plan) of how to meet these quality requirements?
- Is there a representative of the customer present who is responsible for acceptance and is there an acceptance plan?
- Are there procedures, standards and work instructions against which the work can be tested?
- Which quality checks are used in the project?
- Has a Quality Log been set up?
- Has a product-based plan been drawn up (Product Breakdown and Product Flow Diagram)?
- Have Product Descriptions been written for the most important deliverables?
- Have the most important deliverables and activities in the various stages been defined?
- Has account been taken in the project of interfaces with other projects and has it been clearly established who is responsible for this and where?
- Have tolerance boundaries been included in the Project Plan with respect to time, money, quality and scope?
- Have priorities for the management elements (quality, time, money and scope) been included in the Project Plan?

- Have milestones and decision points been specified?
- Is there a Business Case and has it been formulated SMART?
- Have tolerances relating to the benefits been included?
- Have the most important risks been identified and evaluated and have countermeasures been defined?
- Have the most important project and business risks been included in the PID?
- Have risk owners been appointed and are there rules for monitoring risks?
- Have the moments for risk analysis and risk management during the project been specified?
- Has a budget been included for dealing with risks?
- Have tolerances for risks been included?
- Have the various reports from the Project Manager to the Project Board been specified?
- Has a clear escalation procedure been defined?
- Has a Communication Plan been included in the PID?
- Has a project file been set up (electronically and physically)?
- Is there authorisation for who has access to which information?
- Has it been established how the project file is to be managed?
- Have the agreements regarding configuration management been clearly recorded?
- Has a configuration management database been set up?
- Are the agreements regarding the change procedure and the exception procedure clearly recorded?
- Has a change authority been appointed and has a change budget been set aside?
- Has an Issue Log been set up?
- Has a PID been written for the project?
- Has the project definition been included in full in the PID?
- Is the project objective SMART?
- Are the deliverables clearly described in the PID?
- Has an End Stage Report been drawn up for the initiation stage?
- Has a Stage Plan been drawn up for the first implementation stage?
- Has the Project Board approved the PID and the Stage Plan for the first execution stage?
- Has the Project Board approved the End Stage Report for the initiation stage?
- Has the budget needed for carrying out the project been approved?
- Have the people and resources required for the first execution stage been released?
- Have there been regular meetings between the Project Manager and the Project Board during the initiation stage?
- Are the Project Board members really the project owners?
- Is there a support base and commitment for the project and for the outcome?

7.3.3 Executing a project
- Was there a kick off?
- Has the Project Manager assigned the work SMART to the Team Managers?
- Have Product Descriptions been written for the most important deliverables?
- Have plans been made at such a detailed level that work can be delegated and checked?
- Is every employee aware of the procedures, standards and work instructions that apply to him/her?
- Do regular Checkpoint Reports and/or progress meetings take place with the Team Managers and are these effective?
- Is the status of the work regularly updated?
- Are the intervals between the reports aligned to the duration times of the deliverables and can these reports be used to effectively correct the progress of the work?

- Do project team members bring up project risks and points for attention and are these recorded and assessed?
- Is there a log kept of attention points and is structured action taken on these attention points?
- Is the status of the work reviewed regularly and the actions that result from this set in motion?
- When reviewing the work are the uncertainties within the project anticipated pro-actively and is use made of the Risk Log to do this?
- Are new uncertainties recorded in the Risk Log and analysed?
- Is the planning adjusted regularly?
- Is there a change procedure and does it work effectively?
- Is there a classification made of the importance of the proposed changes?
- Is there a clear change authority?
- Are the correct documents and products always being used in the project?
- Is the status of all the products and documents fixed and are all the stakeholders aware of this?
- When approved changes are made, are the relevant configuration and associated Product Description altered too?
- Are the deliverables checked/tested before the following activities start?
- Are the users and other suppliers included in the quality reviews?
- Are the deliverables formally handed over and accepted by the Project Manager before these products are released for follow-on activities/use?
- Are Off-Specifications recorded according to a set procedure and does this procedure work effectively?
- Does the Project Board work in practice as it should?
- Do good consultations take place between the Senior User and the various users?
- Are (additional) demands by the users and under the responsibility of the Senior User, made in good time, clearly and sufficiently specific?
- Are the people and resources required available and guaranteed by the Senior Supplier?
- Has a separate Project Evaluation been set up on both the customer's side and that of the supplier and do they work as they should?
- Were specific no go/go moments specified during the execution of the project?
- Is every stage preceded by an explicit and formal 'go' from the Project Board?
- Is an End Stage Report compiled for every stage?
- Did the Project Board discharge the Project Manager from the completed stages on the basis of End Stage Reports?
- Is a separate Stage Plan drawn up before the start of each new stage and is it also approved for the 'go' of the new stage and are the resources required actually released?
- Is the Project Plan (and the risks in the project) updated at stage boundaries?
- Is the technical and financial viability of the project reviewed at stage boundaries?
- Are the lessons learned recorded for each stage and is the work adjusted accordingly?
- Does the Project Manager report regularly to the Project Board members and other stakeholders and does this work effectively?
- Are Project Board meetings held at regular intervals?
- Have clear tolerances been agreed between the Project Board and the Project Manager?
- Have there been escalations in the project and did the Project Manager respond effectively to these: did escalation to the Project Board take place in good time or not until the tolerances had already been exceeded?
- Has the Lessons Learned Log been set up and is it kept up-to-date?

7.3.4 Closing a Project

- Do all the people involved know in good time that the project is to be closed?
- Have all the production resources and facilities currently in use been cancelled in good time or taken out of lease?
- Has the project organisation been disbanded and has a good closure of the project taken place?
- Have all the project team members returned safely to their parent organisation or been assigned to another project?
- Have the files been updated and has the project file been closed and handed over?
- Have all the specialist documents been updated and handed over to the management organisation?
- Has the configuration management database been updated and handed over to the management organisation?
- Have the deliverables been delivered to and accepted by the user organisation and by the management organisation?
- Has proper management of the deliverables and services been arranged?
- Have Follow-On Action Recommendations been made and have all the outstanding Project Issues been handed over to the relevant organisations?
- Has a date been set for the post-project review and has a Post Project Review Plan been drawn up and handed over to the Executive?
- Has a final evaluation been held?
- Has a Lessons Learned Report been compiled and handed over to the relevant customer and supplier organisations?
- Has the relevant costing been done and the indicators handed over to the relevant organisations?
- Has an End Project Report been compiled and handed over to the Project Board, and does it contain a good justification for what has been delivered and an account of the course of the project?
- Has the Project Board discharged the Project Manager on the basis of the End Project Report?

7.4 Sample development of a Project Brief

7.4.1 Project Brief for Garden Shed

Purpose of Project Brief
The Project Brief must provide a complete and sound basis for the start of the process Initiating a Project.

Background
- The family lives on 500m2 of freehold land.
- The family wants to work more in the garden and needs more garden tools for which there is no more room in the garage.

Project objective
- Storage of garden furniture and garden tools so that they are out of sight and dry in the winter.
- To be able to do small garden jobs (for example, repotting plants) in a dry, sheltered place.

Scope
Clearing the ground in the garden where the garden shed is to be built, purchasing and erecting the garden shed and purchasing additional garden tools.

Most important project outcome
- Garden shed erected with lighting, connected to the electricity network.
- Extra garden tools, housed in the garden shed.

Exclusions
- Existing plants do not need to be moved: we will do that ourselves.
- We will move the tools and garden furniture we already have into the garden shed ourselves at a later date.

Constraints
- Maximum available budget € 1000.
- The garden shed must be erected and everything must be ready within 6 weeks because we are giving a barbecue then.

Relationship with other projects
- In 2 weeks time we will also be improving the garden fences. We're doing this together with the neighbours. We cannot erect the garden shed that weekend.

Outline of Business Case
By doing garden maintenance ourselves, we won't need to employ a gardener so often. If the garden furniture can be stored through the winter in the garden shed, the furniture will last a few years longer. Apart from the pleasure we will get from working in the garden, we should be able to recoup the purchase and erection costs of the garden shed pretty quickly.

Quality expectations
- It has to look nice.
- It must not take up too much room.
- We must be able to work in it (repotting plants, etc.).
- The garden shed must be environment friendly, sturdy and maintenance-free.

Acceptance Criteria
- With one or more windows and a sloping roof.
- No more than 8m2, preferably rectangular.
- A small workbench on one side and lighting.
- The shed must be made of hard wood that carries an environmental certificate.

Known risks
- Delivery time, causing the shed to be delivered too late.
- Incorrect delivery, where materials are incomplete or even have to be returned, resulting in lost working days.
- Poor weather, such that we are unable to work on that day.

Highlights of Project Plan
- Order next weekend, clear the ground for building and erecting in the third weekend and paint in the final weekend. We will be able to move the plants ourselves in the first or second weekend.
- The total cost is estimated at € 750 for the garden shed and another € 200 for the garden tools. € 50 to be kept for small items and incidentals.

7.5 Lessons learned

Project management is an art. It is a craft that above all has to be learned by applying and doing. Although every project is unique and so not everything can be taken over from one project to the next, it is still possible to learn during a project and from projects. In PRINCE2 this is explicitly included in the project process by updating lessons learned after every stage and by writing a Lessons Learned Report in the process Closing a Project.

Learning from projects starts as soon as a 'possible' project is mentioned. After all, it is the objective of the process Starting Up a Project to establish whether a potential project is viable and worthwhile. To discover this, a few critical questions must be asked of the Executive in the first place, but of course of all the other stakeholders too. Too often odd jobs or items are thrust into becoming projects, without sufficient questions being asked about whether there is enough basis to start the project or with the project being started without completing the necessary conditions for starting a project. Unfortunately, these often turn out to be expensive lessons.

Well begun is half done. But lessons should be learned from events throughout the project too. These lessons may be about the deliverables, but could also be about the process in the project. Making adjustments on the basis of experience gained and lessons learned can contribute a great deal to the efficiency and effectiveness of projects and must be a permanent part of managing projects. If possible, lessons learned can be applied immediately in the project. At the same time, lessons learned that could be of interest to other projects are handed over to the organisation concerned that initiates and manages these projects. For example, a different test method for deliverables may directly lead to a better insight into the quality of these products or to a different production method.

In projects, lessons learned must be recorded at intervals in a Lessons Learned Log. The Lessons Learned Log must be updated at least at the end of a stage to ensure that interim lessons learned are not forgotten and to ensure that the experience gained in one stage can be applied in the next. At the end of the project the Lessons Learned Report is written based on a final evaluation of the project. The Lessons Learned Log is a useful tool here.

Whether time is set aside for reflection, evaluation and passing on lessons learned depends greatly on a number of factors, such as the organisation's view of learning and the extent to which Project Managers are permitted to make mistakes and learn from them. The process Closing a Project shows clearly that writing a Lessons Learned Report is an implicit part of the project. It is, of course, the case that those involved in the project can learn without a formal evaluation having to take place. By building up personal experience, they will be able to tackle things better next time. A good evaluation, however, ensures a systematic approach and therefore produces valuable information in the short term and for more people. A list of recommendations for a project evaluation is given below:
- Do not wait too long before holding an evaluation. The more time that elapses between the delivery of the result and the evaluation, the less those involved will be able to remember.
- Reserve time and resources (budget) explicitly for the evaluation.
- Where possible, make use of an independent chairman.
- Make sure that the atmosphere around the evaluation is positive. Do not look for scapegoats or guilty parties if projects have failed or overrun.
- Separate people and actions; keep on asking what the other means exactly; show appreciation for comments and realise that 'feelings are valid'.
- Make sure that SMART points for improvement are recorded and shared with all those involved. Agree on what should be done with the lessons learned.

To learn from experience and turn the lessons learned into a different way of working and/or approach, the Project Manager and the team need to hold regular (interim) evaluations. All team members ought to take part in these evaluations.

The checklist below sums up the subjects that come up in such an evaluation.
- Did everyone have a clear idea of the objective?
- How do you evaluate the quality of the team's (interim) results?
- How was the composition of the team?
- Was the approach and task distribution suitable for this task?
- How was the internal reporting and documentation?
- How was the project control?
- Was the available time well planned and monitored?
- As a team, are we using the most suitable form of decision-making?
- Did everyone take an active part?
- Was the correct management style used?
- Were feelings and opinions discussed openly?
- How do you assess the effectiveness of the teamwork in general?
- Did you work comfortably as a member of this team?
- How do you assess the way you functioned and your role in the team?

All these questions are points for attention to be able to evaluate the conduct of the project. The responses will all contain information to record experiences, to learn from them and thus to improve one's own way of working and that of others.

7.6 Filing structure

It is important to maintain a fixed filing structure for setting up and archiving project documents. This helps to prevent stored documents from being difficult to find at a later date. At the same time, a fixed filing structure makes it easy to take over a colleague's work, should circumstances make this necessary.

It is recommended that a separate structure for management products and specialist products be set up: the specialist file and the management file.

7.6.1 Management files

The management file consists of all the documents and products necessary to be able to manage the project. This file is subdivided into:
- Project file
- Stage files
- Quality file

The project file contains all documents that relate to the project as a whole:
- Project management structure and the associated job descriptions.
- Project plan (including the deliverables).
- Business Case, including the updates.
- Risk Log, including the updates.
- PID, including the updates.
- Project closure documents such as the delivery protocols, the End Project Report, the post-project report, etc.

The stage file contains all documents that relate to a specific stage:
- Stage organisation chart with information about the team members.
- Stage Plan, any team plans and the Exception Plans.
- Control documents: copies of the authorisation for the Work Packages, Checkpoint Reports, Highlight Reports, Exception Reports and reports on the evaluation of the Exception Plan and the End Stage Assessment.
- Correspondence, such as letters, memos, other reports of conversations, notes, etc.
- Daily Log.

The project has the same number of stage files as stages.

The quality file contains all correspondence directly related to controlling the quality of the project deliverables:
- The Project Quality Plan, including the Configuration Management Plan.
- The configuration items database, with at least Product Description(s) of the deliverables.
- Inspection documents, such as inspection reports, test results, audit reports, etc., but also the invitations to reviews to be held and the lists of agreements.
- Quality Log. This should clearly show (preferably in the form of a table) who carried out which quality control, what the result was and any actions taken.
- Issue Log, subdivided into Requests for Change, Off-Specifications and other Project Issues.

7.6.2 Specialist file

The specialist file contains all the technical documentation relating to the specialist products in the project. These may be designs, drawings, manuals, questionnaires and training material. The layout is determined to a great extent by the various deliverables.

In addition to the product-related documentation, a section on general correspondence is usually included for correspondence or external information that does not refer to a specific configuration item. When an Off-Specification is discovered, a copy of the Exception Report is stored in the specialist file with the configuration item in question.

8. Further Information

8.1 Recommended PRINCE2 literature

Managing Successful Projects with PRINCE2   **ISBN 0113308914**
The handbook includes process descriptions and approaches to project management as seen by PRINCE2. Moreover, the handbook contains hints and tips and includes example of products and forms.

Passing the PRINCE2 Examinations   **ISBN 0113309120**
This book serves as an aid when studying for the Foundation and Practitioner exams.

Management of Risk: guidance for Practitioners   **ISBN 0113309090**
This book is an OGC publication, based on 'best practice' and describes the management of risks in projects and programmes.

Managing Successful Programmes   **ISBN 0113309171**
This book is an OGC publication and describes the programme management structure and methods of approach. The methodology is in keeping with the PRINCE2 method.

How to manage Business Change   **ISBN 1903091101**
This book is an OGC publication and describes the most important attention points when implementing change.

Business Benefits through Project Management   **ISBN 0113308981**
This book describes how organisations can secure the necessary project management skills in their company processes and culture.

8.2 Contact addresses

OGC
Rosebery Court, St Andrew's Business Park
Norwich, Norfolk, NR7 0HS
United Kingdom
Telephone   : +44 (0)845 000 4999.
E-mail   : ServiceDesk@ogc.gsi.gov.uk
URL   : http://www.ogc.gov.uk

The APM Group Ltd
Attn. Richard Pharro
7-8 Queen Square
High Wycombe, Buckinghamshire, HP11 2BP
United Kingdom
Telephone   : +44(0) 1494 452450
Fax   : +44(0) 1494 459559
E-mail   : info@apmgroup.co.uk
URL   : http://www.apmgroup.co.uk

EXIN

Godebaldkwartier 365
3511 DT UTRECHT
The Netherlands
Telephone : +31 (0)30 234 48 58
Fax : +31 (0) 30 234 31 11
E-mail : info@exin-exams.com
URL : http://www.exin-exams.com

The PRINCE User Group Ltd (UK)

c/o Intracite Ltd
Unit A, Watchmoor Trade Centre
Watchmoor Road
Camberly Surrey, GU15 3AJ
United Kingdom
Telephone : +44 (0)1276 686363
E-mail : admin@usergroup.org.uk
URL : http://prince.usergroup.org.uk

IPMA

Postbus 1167
3860 BD NIJKERK
Telephone : +31 (0)33 247 3430
Fax : +31 (0)33 246 0470
E-mail : info@ipma.ch
URL : http://www.ipma.ch